● **Everything You Need to Know About Designing Effective Learning Games**

Play to Learn

SHARON BOLLER
and KARL KAPP

ATD Press is an internationally renowned source of insightful and practical information on talent development, workplace learning, and professional development.

Information and images for the Feed the World and TE Town case studies in chapter 6 are courtesy of The Mosaic Company and TE Connectivity, respectively.

ATD Press
1640 King Street
Alexandria, VA 22314 USA

Ordering information: Books published by ATD Press can be purchased by visiting ATD's website at www.td.org/books or by calling 800.628.2783 or 703.683.8100.

Library of Congress Control Number: 2017930322
ISBN-10: 1-56286-577-3
ISBN-13: 978-1-56286-577-1
e-ISBN: 978-1-56286-772-0

ATD Press Editorial Staff
Director: Kristine Luecker
Manager: Christian Green
Community of Practice Manager, Learning Technologies: Justin Brusino
Developmental Editor: Jack Harlow
Associate Editor: Caroline Coppel
Cover Design: Derek Thornton, Faceout Studio
Text Design: Francelyn Fernandez and Maggie Hyde
Printed by BR Printers, San Jose, CA

Contents

Preface

Mind-blowing.

That was the one-word description a player gave a few years ago when asked to share his reaction to a learning game called A Paycheck Away. The feedback perfectly captured the "why" of learning games. Most of us have not heard learners use the adjective *mind-blowing* to describe their reaction to any other sort of learning activity we've developed. Clearly, for this learner, the learning game he played had achieved its potential. It gained and kept his attention, fully immersing him in a learning experience.

There is a large body of research that shows that games are more effective than lecture-based approaches to learning. In addition, games offer compelling ways to help people learn strategy, resource allocation, and innovative thinking. They can help people understand alternative points of view. They provide an opportunity for each learner to have a personalized learning experience in which the learner can choose to review content, attempt different strategies, experiment, and experience the game differently from co-workers and still reach the same learning outcome. On the more mundane issue of simply remembering key knowledge, such as product facts, industry information, and process steps, learning games can provide critical spacing and repetition of content, which helps cement memory.

If you're reading this book, you probably already believe that games can be effective learning tools. Your challenge is in execution, and that's where *Play to Learn* can help. Instructional design and game design are different disciplines. Most instructional designers and training professionals do not possess game design skills or even game literacy, which is knowledge of game lingo and structure. This book will help you systematically acquire game literacy and build learning-game design skills.

The methodology and process we cover in *Play to Learn* is what we use and teach to others in workshops we've conducted over the last several years (Figure I-1). As you go through the book, you'll see that it progresses through the nine steps, devoting a chapter to each one. We show as well as tell, and we provide you with lots of "work on your own" activities to help you build your skills in learning-game design. Chapter 1 introduces you to some basic game lingo, such as what a game is and common game design terminology. Chapters 2 through 5 take you through the first four steps of our process. You'll learn how to play and evaluate commercial and learning games, the basic instructional design requirements you need to have in place before you begin designing your game, and the game design components you need to plot out. Chapter 6 provides you with case studies of two learning games, breaking down their instructional design and their game design. Chapters 7 through 11 then take you through the remaining steps in the process, guiding you from your first game prototype through deployment of a learning game. Chapter 12 summarizes the entire experience and how to move forward in creating more learning games.

Figure I-1. The 9-Step Process to Learning-Game Design and Development

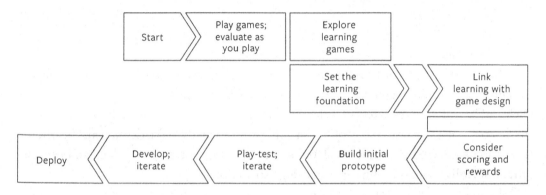

Many designers ask the question, "When should I use games for learning?" Armed with the skills you gain in this book, you can shift the conversation to, "Which games should I use for this specific learning situation?" You will have the skills to design and develop games for all types of contexts and situations, from a simple, experiential game to a much more complex digital game or tabletop simulation. You, too, will be able to develop a learning experience that a player describes as "mind-blowing."

Sharon Boller and Karl Kapp
March 2017

Part 1

Playing Games to Learn About Games

The Basics

In This Chapter

✓ What is a game?

✓ What is the difference between "play" and a "game"?

✓ What game lingo do you need to know?

✓ Guru game play opportunity

What Is a Game?

It seems like a simple question: "What is a game?" But when you think about it, there are many variations on what is called a "game": Simple activities like tic-tac-toe, card games like Go Fish or poker, and board games like Monopoly and Stratego. Mobile games like Angry Birds, and console games like the *Assassin's Creed* series. Even large-scale, complicated computer-generated game worlds like *World of Warcraft* or *EVE Online,* and live sports games like soccer or lacrosse.

So asking "What is a game?" isn't so simple.

When you dig deeper, games of all kinds tend to have certain elements in common. The commonalities among different types of games can be studied and used for designing a learning game. Stop for a moment and write down your definition of the term *game.*

The definition of the term *game* is:

How did you do? Did your definition include the concept of fun? Did it include the idea of competition, of winners and losers? Did it include rules or goals? While there may not be a perfect definition that covers all types of games, here is the one we use:

A game is an activity that has a **goal,** a **challenge** (or challenges), and **rules** that guide achievement of the goal; **interactivity** with either other players or the **game environment** (or both); and **feedback mechanisms** that give clear cues as to how well or poorly you are performing. It results in a **quantifiable outcome** (you win or lose, you hit the target, and so on) that usually generates an **emotional reaction** in players.

Let's examine each bolded element to see how it supports the idea of a game.

- **Goal:** One difference between the terms *play* and *game* is the introduction of a goal. If kids are running around at recess, they are playing. However, the moment one child says to another, "Let's race to the big tree," play changes into a game, because a goal has been introduced. Goals provide a clear outcome and a delineation of completion. They are an important element in all types of games, especially learning games.
- **Challenge:** The challenge in a game could be against another player, the game itself, or your own high score from the last time you played. A game without a challenge can be boring, but a game with too much challenge is frustrating. Learning-game designers need to strike a balance between providing a challenge and supporting the players' ability to quickly and easily master the game.
- **Rules:** Rules are the structure that creates the game space and gives all players an equal chance of succeeding. Learning-game designers should strive to create simple, easy-to-understand rules that contribute to the learning outcome of the game.
- **Interactivity:** Good games provide many opportunities for the players to interact with game content, other players, and the rules of the game. Games that do too much "telling" and not enough decision making or interaction quickly become boring. The higher the level of interactivity created within the game, the more engaged the players and the more likely they will learn from the game.
- **Game Environment:** Every learning game is a self-contained space. The game space—the area in which the players play the game—has its own rules, challenges, and social norms. Some people call the game space a "magic circle," because game design typically includes creating constraints in the form of rules that only work within that circle. Consider Pictionary. It would be far easier if players could simply write

the word they are trying to convey instead of drawing a picture of the word. However, the game space does not allow them to write the word; it only allows them to draw a picture. This rule is particular to the game; in most situations outside the Pictionary game space, if you need to explain an object to someone, you can either say the object's name or write it down. The constraint in Pictionary makes the game challenging and creates an environment different from other social spaces.

- **Feedback Mechanisms:** Games are great tools for providing feedback, because players usually receive feedback immediately. In Monopoly, you can see if you are ahead or behind simply by comparing the number of hotels you have with the number other players have. Feedback is usually unambiguous; players typically know where they stand in relation to the outcome and other players. It also lets players continually adjust their own game play and actions. Immediate feedback and constant adjustments are two game elements that make them great tools for learning.
- **Quantifiable Outcome:** The result of a well-designed game is that players know, without a doubt, whether they have won the game and whether the game is over. There is a clear score, a clear leveling up, or a clear winning state that allows everyone to agree that the game has ended. In contrast, play often has no clear end line or finished state. Instead, people get tired or bored and move on to something else. But games have a clear point at which the game is over. In fact, as players move through the game environment and accomplish goals during the game, they are also moving closer to the state where the game ends.
- **Emotional Reaction:** Often games trigger an emotional response in players as they work through the game's challenges or achieve the game's goal. They may experience fun, frustration, excitement, anger, enthusiasm, happiness, or contentment. Learning-game designers should be conscious of the emotions they hope to evoke and make sure they aren't generating unintended ones (such as anger or frustration).

One element is missing from the above definition: competition. While many games have competition, it is not a defining factor because many excellent games require cooperation. Many people's default idea of a game is one person or team competing against another. But games like Forbidden Island and Pandemic require cooperation. And often, in a work environment, the concept of cooperation and teamwork is a better design for a learning game than competition.

Learning the Lingo of Games

Learning certain lingo in the field of game design will help you effectively communicate with your teammates about the game's design because you will have a common language to express ideas. It will also help you communicate with vendors and others in the field who will be using terms and concepts related to game design and development, especially if you create a game that requires help to design and develop. And finally, learning the lingo helps you when reading other game design books or articles, because this terminology is common to game design.

Game Goal

The game goal is the win state. It's the objective of the game. It's any achievement or activity that ends the game. Without a game goal, you'd have no game.

In a running race, for example, the game goal is to be the first one to cross the finish line. In Monopoly, it is to finish with the most property and cash. In Risk, it is to achieve world domination. In a learning game, it might be to sell more than a million dollars of product, successfully navigate a compliance maze, or correctly identify and eliminate incorrect passwords.

Core Dynamic

The core dynamic is what the players must do to achieve the win state or accomplish the goal; it is tightly linked to the game goal. The core dynamic answers the question, "What do I need to do to win?" When you tell someone about a game, you typically describe it in a sentence or two: "In Risk, you try to take over the most territories and achieve world domination." The core dynamic of Risk, therefore, is territory acquisition.

Players' enjoyment of the core dynamic contributes hugely to their evaluation of how engaging the game is to play. People play a game because they like its core dynamic. This is one reason why some people like one type of game and others like another. Some people like the core dynamic of alignment found in games such as Candy Crush, Timeline, or Bejeweled. Others like a core dynamic of outwitting an opponent, such as in chess or Stratego.

Choosing the right core dynamic is critical to the success of the game. Most games have one to two core dynamics. If you are first starting to design learning games, it's easiest to select one core dynamic and design your game around it. As you add dynamics, you add complexity, and the game can become confusing to the players. They will not understand what they are supposed to do to achieve the game goal.

Table 1-1 describes common core dynamics and identifies specific games in which they're used. Any learning game you design will likely use one or more of these dynamics. Some games have only one, while others may use two or more.

Table 1-1. Descriptions and Examples of Core Dynamics

Core Dynamic	Example
Race to the finish: Get to the finish before anyone else or time runs out.	Life, Candy Land, Mario Kart
Territory acquisition: Acquire or take land, typically to create an empire or own the most of something.	Risk, Catan, Monopoly
Exploration: Wander around and check out various aspects of your game world to see if you can find things of value.	*Minecraft, Legend of Zelda*
Collecting: Find and acquire specified objects.	Trivial Pursuit, Checkers
Rescue or escape: Get out of a situation or place.	*City of Heroes,* Forbidden Island, Capture the Flag
Alignment: Arrange game pieces in a particular order.	Tic-Tac-Toe, Connect 4
Forbidden act: Get fellow players to break the rules, make a wrong move, or do something they shouldn't.	Twister, Operation, Great Divide
Construct or build: Create something using specified resources.	*The Sims, Roller Coaster Tycoon,* Jenga
Outwit: Use specialized knowledge or skills to defeat an opponent.	Stratego, Chess
Solution: Solve a problem or puzzle.	SpellTower, *The Room, Portal,* Clue
Matching: Recognize things that are alike or that fit a specific description; create pairs or groupings.	Spot It!, Guess Who, Go Fish!

Game Mechanics

Game mechanics are the rules. In some games, the rules are specifically for the players. In other games, mostly online games, there are rules that govern the game system. The game mechanics define how people achieve the game goal.

Game mechanics interact to determine the complexity and flow of the game. A mechanic might be how turns are taken, how players move pieces across the game board, or how much damage players can take before they lose a life.

Mechanics are important in players' perception of the game. A game may have a great game goal but crummy rules, so the game won't be engaging. When you play a game, evaluate how the rules contribute to your engagement with the game and how those rules are structured to make it harder or easier to accomplish the game goal.

Game Elements

Game elements are the features or components that enhance the game play experience and help immerse the players in the game. Elements can range from the visual aesthetics of the game to the weight of the pieces or the arrangement of the cards. The consistency and alignment of the game elements help create its theme and "look and feel." Table 1-2 lists and defines common game elements.

Table 1-2. Common Game Elements

Element
Aesthetics: The visual look of the game and the various game parts.
Chance: Elements you include to equalize the playing experience, add an element of surprise, or derail players. Chance can be useful; it can often be unintentional.
Competition: Players oppose one another, with one player attempting to gain the advantage over another.
Conflict: Something the player has to overcome; something to be conquered or to create a sense of urgency.
Cooperation: Players work together to achieve a goal, or at least manage a challenge within the game.
Levels: A game can be organized into levels of play to allow players to go from novice to mastery or to allow players from different experience levels to play the same game. Levels typically indicate a progression of difficulty through a game.
Resources: Assets such as money or objects that help a player gain an advantage. Typically, resources can be acquired or lost during a game, with some resources allocated to a player at the start.
Rewards: Achievements players earn based on performance or completion.
Story: A narrative that weaves throughout an entire game or sets up the reason you are playing the game and elaborates on the theme.
Strategy: Elements you include to force the player to analyze and consider various options. It gives the player high control over the game's outcome.
Theme: A backdrop for a game. A theme might be "surviving in space," "fighting zombies," or "becoming a gunslinger in the Wild West."
Time: In a game, time can be compressed (something that would take hours or days can take minutes), serve as a resource that players can gain and lose, or be a complete nonfactor. It can also be integrated into the game goal, with players racing against time to win the game.

An Example: Monopoly

Let's take a quick look at the game Monopoly and map it to the lingo just covered (Table 1-3).

Table 1-3. Definitions of Game Lingo

Term	Monopoly Example
Game Goal	• Finish the game with the most property and cash
Core Dynamics	• Collection (you collect properties) • Territory acquisition (you form monopolies)
Game Mechanics (a sample of the rules)	• You collect $200 every time you pass Go. • If you land on a space owned by someone else, you pay that player rent. • If your opponent fails to ask you for the rent before the next player rolls the dice, you do not have to pay rent. • You must own all properties within a color grouping before you can purchase houses. • You must purchase four houses before you can purchase a hotel.
Game Elements	• **Chance:** Dice rolls determine what space you land on, which, in turn, affects what you can buy or what you might have to pay out in rent. You can draw Chance or Community Chest cards. Depending on what card you draw, you may have a good or bad event happen. • **Competition:** You are working to defeat your opponents. • **Cooperation:** You can work out deals with your competitors to acquire property or make trades. • **Strategy:** Most players develop a preferred strategy for winning. Some opt to acquire utilities and railroads. Others want to occupy Boardwalk and Park Place. Still others negotiate special terms in exchange for trading away a specific property. • **Aesthetics:** The visual look of the board has inspired a wide range of spin-offs, such as college-themed versions of the game. • **Conflict:** You often get into head-to-head conflicts with other players. Many a game has ended in anger as people's frustrations with one another supersede any enjoyment. • **Time:** Monopoly's instructions offer a timed version of the game, in which players compete for 45 minutes to see who's richest at the end of the period.

Guru Game Play Opportunity

To help reinforce the information and concepts in this book, we have created an online game for you to play called Game Design Guru. Figure 1-1 is an image from the game.

Throughout this book, you'll be directed to play different levels of the game; the levels correspond with certain chapters. They provide a great opportunity to reinforce your knowledge while seeing an example of a learning game and how it gets incorporated into a larger learning endeavor (such as reading this book and completing the other activities within it).

The first level is about the game lingo discussed in this chapter. Create a game account at www.theknowledgeguru.com/ATDGameDesignGuru and start playing to learn!

If you prefer to play on your phone, you can. However, we recommend you first create a game account using your laptop or tablet. Then download the phone app for either Android or iOS by searching for "KGuru Quest," a mobile version of the game.

Figure 1-1. Screenshot From Game Design Guru

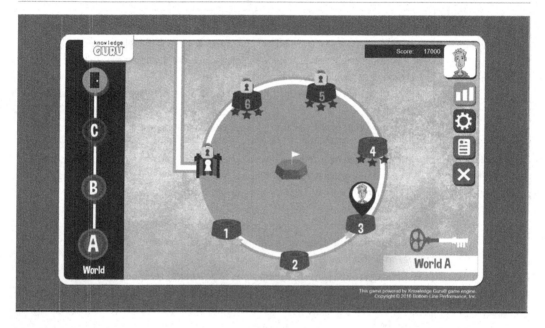

Wrap-Up

You are now armed with the basics you need to get started on your game design journey. The next chapter introduces the steps involved in becoming a learning-game designer. (Spoiler alert: One of the first things you need to do to start the game design process is play lots of games!)

Playing Entertainment Games

In This Chapter
✓ Overview of the learning-game design process
✓ Why do you need to play games?
✓ What's the difference between digital and tabletop games?
✓ What makes a game engaging?
✓ Work on your own

This book evolved from the learning-game design workshop we have been teaching for the past three years. In that workshop, we help people build skill in learning-game design by following a process, as shown in Figure 2-1. This book takes you through that process.

Figure 2-1. Learning-Game Design Process: Play and Evaluate

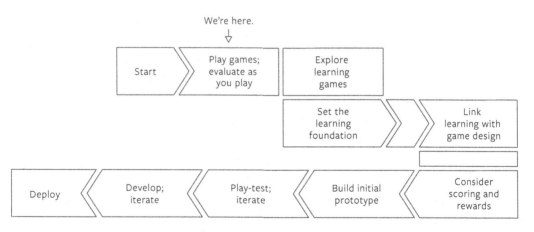

Note that our process starts with game play—and evaluating the games you play. That's what this chapter is all about.

Why You Have to Play Games

Chapter 1 introduced you to the lingo of games. This chapter will introduce you to the game design process. It also provides direction on how to execute the first step of the process: Play games, lots of them. Learning-game design is a bit like writing a book: Most authors read hundreds or even thousands of books before they ever attempt to write one. They become terrific readers before they become good writers.

Similarly, to design a strong learning game, you start by playing and evaluating lots of different games. Doing so helps you:

- **Identify what makes games fun—or not—for the target audience.** To maximize your learning experience in this step, play games that both do and do not include you as the target audience. You often won't be designing a learning game that is targeted to you, so explore games designed to appeal to a wide array of personalities and interests.
- **Learn the lingo of games.** This includes how various game design elements are used to keep players engaged.
- **Get ideas on game elements, rules, and dynamics to use.** Playing games will likely trigger ideas of how you could use their concepts within a learning game. There is a reason that so many *Jeopardy!* clones exist in classrooms: Most people have watched *Jeopardy!* on TV and enjoyed it. It's an easy game to mimic when designing a workshop and creating a recall activity. However, you can go well beyond *Jeopardy!* if you take the time to play different games.
- **Learn what's possible.** By playing games, you'll learn to recognize different game formats and types, such as board games, card games, dice games, PC games, console games, mobile games, experiential games, improv games, role-playing games, games of chance, and games of strategy. The world of games is massive; exploring a wide array of game types will dramatically expand your ability to brainstorm ideas and be creative in your designs.

What Kinds of Games to Play?

You have many choices about what kinds of games to play. We recommend you play games that are part of two broad categories: digital and tabletop (Figure 2-2). By playing both types, you can evaluate the pros and cons of each and become more knowledgeable about your own capabilities to produce each kind of game. You'll find that each type differs in how it explains the rules, incorporates story and aesthetics, and manages scoring and complexity. Compare and contrast how game designers handle these game design decisions.

Figure 2-2. Two Major Categories of Games and Their Game Types

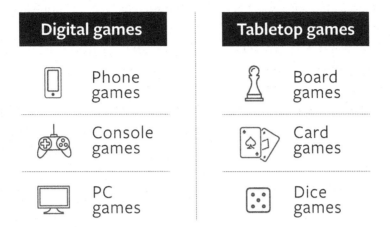

Digital Games

Digital games are what many training professionals want to produce because they want an e-learning solution. This section overviews two major types of digital games: mobile games and console and PC games. Playing games in this category gives you an idea of these games' sophistication levels and how playing experiences differ within each subcategory. If your target learners play these kinds of games, you'll also need to play them to understand what the experience is like for them and what factors engage them.

Mobile Games

We consider mobile games ones designed for smartphones first. These games are often designed to be played in short spurts of a few minutes at a time. As you play them, pay attention to:

- Complexity of graphics; use and readability of the text.
- Choices on when to use text and when to use images.
- Navigation and how it helps players figure out where to go and what to do next.
- Use of play to teach play as opposed to a bunch of text "tells" that precede game play.
- Use of levels to mark progression of play.
- Achievements and scoring.
- How replay is encouraged through the scoring system. For example, Angry Birds, a classic phone game, awards you up to three stars for each level you complete. If you figure out the solution but require numerous steps to do it, you get one star. If you whizz through the problem, you get three stars. To improve your star rating, you can retry the level.

Console and PC Games

This category could be broken apart, but let's keep it together for play evaluation purposes. This category includes many different genres, including role-playing games, puzzle games, sports games, multiplayer games, adventure games, and strategy games. As you play, note:

- **Use of graphics and animation:** These games tend to be graphically and aesthetically rich and generate a "wow" reaction in players.
- **Use of 3-D environments:** Not all these games are 3-D, but it is worth experiencing some that are to see how immersive and realistic they can feel.
- **Use of sound and sound effects:** How do these elements help immerse you in the story?
- **Extensive use of story and theme:** These games are often designed for hours of play at a time. Many within this grouping are not "casual," which simply means it isn't possible to casually pick them up and then walk away. They are meant to provide hours of immersion and entertainment.
- **How you feel as you play:** The immersive graphics, sounds, and game play can ratchet up your emotions quite a bit. You may feel stressed, excited, victorious, or scared.
- **Multiplayer options:** How does getting to play with someone else affect your experience?

Because many games are designed to be playable across different platforms, you may find you can download a game originally designed for a console or PC to your tablet device. The game may have been altered to fit this format, but you can sometimes still get the essence of the experience.

Try playing a new game every week. Make sure you play games through more than a level or two so you truly get a sense of their complexity and richness.

Tabletop Games

If you opt to include games in a live workshop setting, the likely format is going to be some type of tabletop game. The most common tabletop format is the board game, but it can also include dice games or card games. Many of us grew up playing Life, Monopoly, Aggravation, or Risk. Your task is to get beyond the Milton Bradley family of board games and explore more creative ones such as Ticket to Ride, New York 1901, Forbidden Island, and Mine Shift.

Compare casual party games such as Apples to Apples, Cards Against Humanity, or Pictionary with more involved strategy-based tabletop games such as Settlers of Catan or Pandemic. Becoming a learning-game designer means increasing your knowledge beyond game shows or childhood board games. These games can entertain, but there are other more creative games available. Even choosing three to six lesser-known games and playing them vastly expands your frame of reference.

Table 2-1 lists tabletop and digital games we recommend for play and evaluation. They represent a broad variety of game types within the genre. Play several. If cost is an issue, check out a local game store and see what they have that you can try without buying. Most game stores allow you to play before buying. You can also watch demos of games on YouTube, but this should be your last option; playing is far more effective than watching a demo. You won't have an emotional reaction from watching a demo, which is key to understanding what makes a game engaging. Also, try your local library, which may have games you can check out.

Table 2-1. Ideas for Games You Can Play and Evaluate

Phone Games	PC or Tablet Games	Console Games	Tabletop Games
• Angry Birds • Cut the Rope • Plants vs. Zombies • Candy Crush • Fallout Shelter • Lara Croft GO • Two Dots • Scallywags • Pokémon GO	• *Civilization* • *SimCity* (or other *Sims* title) • Jackbox games (project from a tablet or PC onto a TV screen) • Tablet versions of Settlers of Catan, Pandemic, or Forbidden Island	• Madden sports games • *Wii Golf* or *Wii Bowling* • *Skyrim* • Jackbox games • *Uncharted* series • *Assassin's Creed* series • *Portal* (PC and console)	• Fluxx (cards) • Fuse (dice, cards) • Settlers of Catan • Mineshaft • New York 1901 • Ticket to Ride • Spot It! • Timeline • Pandemic • Forbidden Island

The Engagement Factor

When you evaluate the games, pay attention to what makes them engaging to play. We've deliberately chosen not to ask "What makes it fun?" but instead "What makes it engaging?" People often think of the words *fun* and *entertainment* as synonyms. However, learning games aren't typically about entertaining people. While a learning game may be fun in an entertaining way, it doesn't have to in order to be effective. It does have to be engaging. The players need to be involved and vested in the activity, expending energy, thought, and focus. If the game is on a work topic they consider to be a serious one (safety, compliance, risk), they may be fully engaged and learning, but not having fun as people sometimes think of it.

Kevin Werbach, a professor in the Wharton School at the University of Pennsylvania, has a Coursera course on gamification. In it, he lists several qualities that make a game fun. They include winning, achieving goals, triumphing, collaborating, exploring, collecting, building, problem solving, strategizing, being surprised, role playing, and imagining (Werbach n.d.). This list is helpful because it goes beyond the simple word *fun* to get people thinking about what makes something fun.

Table 2-2 organizes these qualities and provides our thoughts on what makes each one engaging. The left column identifies activities people might find fun to do in a game. The middle column explains what makes them mentally engaging (our goal with a learning game). The right column identifies implications to consider when you incorporate the activity into a learning game.

Table 2-2. Linking Fun to Learning

Game Activities People Find Fun	What Makes Them Engaging	Implications for Learning Games

• Grapple with challenges.
• Triumph over a challenge after working at it.
• Achieve something (a win state, a trophy, a new level).
• Figure out solutions to problems.
• Create strategies that lead to a win or resolution of a challenge.
	• Mental satisfaction of overcoming adversity or some difficulty.
	• Sensation of mastery and accomplishment.
	• Mental stimulation; using their brains and savvy to find a solution.
	• Compatibility with many people's natural tendency to be goal oriented.
		• Thoughtful incorporation of goals, challenges, and adversity can be linked to real-world job situations:
		  ☐ Goals are everywhere in the work world: sales goals, productivity goals, safety goals, retention goals.
		  ☐ Challenges abound in the workplace: time, money, and resource management; economic challenges; adverse event challenges; innovation challenges.
		  ☐ Problem solving and strategizing are higher-order skills that many knowledge workers and companies need more of. Games become a useful way of encouraging this type of thinking, if it's required for the job.

• Earn the title of "winner."	• Feeling of well-being and pride that comes from the admiration and recognition that winners and achievers often receive.	• Having employees that feel valued and recognized is critical to sustaining engagement. You can leverage this need in your game's design.
• Collect, explore, or escape.	• Being active mentally stimulates us and keeps us from feeling bored or distracted. • Feeling of accomplishment; this is closely linked to goal achievement. • Action often generates an emotional response. Emotion interests us.	• Engagement in a learning activity is typically measured by how involved a learner gets; activity-based elements tend to generate more involvement than passive ones, such as reading or watching. If mental activity and physical actions are required of us, it's harder to disengage than if we can remain passive.

Game Activities People Find Fun	What Makes Them Engaging	Implications for Learning Games
• Collaborate with others to work through a challenge or get something done.	• Desire to feel valued by teammates. • Desire not to let someone down (if playing on a team). • Desire for interaction with others. • As with action, interaction often generates an emotional response. Emotion interests us.	• To accomplish goals, people usually have to collaborate with others. Learning games lend themselves well to cooperative play, which helps build collaborative behaviors.
• Role-play or imagine themselves in a different context.	• Desire to feel creative. • Ability to safely explore something we'd normally consider too "out there" to be part of. • Enjoyment of pretending or imagining; it can be very freeing.	• In the workplace, mistakes can be costly. Allowing people to role-play or imagine in a game is a safe practice area that causes no harm. • Fantasy can also be a useful way of helping workplace learners accept a situation they would otherwise object to as not being realistic enough to fit their specific work world. The fantasy elements make it clear it is not supposed to be an exact representation of their world. • Imagination in game play can also cultivate creativity and innovation, two desirable things in a workplace.

Going Beyond "Fun"

Playing games for enjoyment is different from playing games to evaluate the quality and efficacy of the game design. As you play games, consider the following questions. This list is comprehensive so you can see the full thought process:

- What's the game goal? Is it clear? Is it compelling to you? Why or why not?
- What's the game's core dynamic? Is it a single dynamic or a blend of two, such as collection and race to the finish?
- Are the rules clear? How do players learn them?
- What game mechanics make the game most fun? Which ones would you change? What would happen if you did? (Try changing one of the mechanics and replaying the game to see how it alters the play experience.)
- Do the aesthetics of the game draw you in? What emotional reaction do they elicit?

- Is the game balanced? Does it accommodate different player levels? How?
- Is the game a good match for its target audience?
- Is there a story associated with this game? How does it enhance the game-play experience? How did the designers weave the story throughout the game? If they didn't, why not? Would it add to or detract from the game if they did?
- What's the balance between strategy and chance? How does the chance factor affect how you feel about the game?
- Is the game cooperative, competitive, or a blend of both? Does this increase or decrease your motivation to play?
- If the game is competitive and you lose, how does this make you feel? Does it motivate you to play again, or do you not want to play again to avoid losing?
- If it's a digital game, how easy is it to navigate? How clear is the navigation? Can you quickly learn by exploring?
- Finally, as a learning-game designer, what elements from this game could you use in a game you design?

A Sample Evaluation: Settlers of Catan

Let's go through an in-depth evaluation of a game. Settlers of Catan is an extremely popular board game that has won numerous awards. The evaluation in Table 2-3 mirrors the setup of the Entertainment Game Evaluation Worksheet in appendix 1. It offers an example to help you see what you should pay attention to and analyze as you play.

Table 2-3. Evaluation of Settlers of Catan

What Is the Game Goal?
Be the first person to earn 10 points in the game.
What Core Dynamics Were Used?
Two dynamics are used: building and collecting. You earn points by building things, such as roads, homes, and settlements. You are able to build things by collecting resource cards (sheep, wheat, bricks, wood) and then using those resources to get what you need to build.
List at Least 3 Game Mechanics From the Game
1. You cannot build until you have the right set of resources to use. The types of resources vary, depending on whether you want to build a road, a house, or a settlement.   2. If you roll a 7 and you have more than seven cards in your hand, you must give up half your cards.
3. If you roll a 7, you can move the Robber to any tile on the board you choose. This freezes out those who might have access to the resource specified on the tile.   4. If you build on a port, you can leverage the port to help you accumulate resources faster, exchanging one kind of resource card for another type of resource you need.

Identify and Describe the Game Elements Used in the Game		
Aesthetics Story **Chance** Conflict **Competition** **Cooperation**	Levels **Resources** **Rewards** **Strategy** Theme Time	There are really nice graphics; they evoke the mood and set the stage for play. Some of the cards are hard to distinguish—for example, sheep and wheat are tough to keep straight. Where you can place your starting settlement is based on chance—a role of the dice. There is also a Robber, who gets moved every time someone rolls a 7. Although the game is a competition, it can be tricky to see who is really winning, because people can have Development Cards hidden away that may have earned them points. You can cooperate with others by trading, which is fun. There are four primary resources you need to build, and you earn points based on the quality of what you're building. There are several strategies for winning; the game board is different every time you play, which makes the game play interesting.

What Feedback Did You Get for How You Were Doing?

You could see your progress in building and you had a scorecard that clearly indicated the value of each item. You could also see what other players were doing. However, you could not see the Development Cards other players may have had, which would influence their total score.

What Aspects of This Game Could Inspire Your Learning Game?

Blending cooperation and competition; a nice balance between chance and strategy. If you were creating a project management game, the idea of having to both cooperate and compete to get resources is a good one, as is the idea of collecting resources before you can build anything. Another good idea is a game board that varies game play by letting people reorganize the tiles that comprise it, which encourages repeat plays.

Other Notes

The game is complex to learn. It's best if someone already knows how to play. Barring that, expect to spend an hour playing a game and figuring it out as you go. Subsequent plays are much easier and very fun. People who don't normally like playing games would find this too difficult to learn unless one of the players already had expertise and could shorten the learning process for others.

Work on Your Own

Plants vs. Zombies is a hugely popular game that game designers often tout as an example of good game design. You can download a free version from either Google Play or the App Store. Play through it for 10 to 15 minutes, and then complete a game evaluation worksheet (in appendix 1 or at www.td.org/PlaytoLearnExtras). Once you finish, flip to appendix 2 and compare your answers with ours.

Wrap-Up

This chapter walked you through the process of playing and evaluating entertainment games. The next step in your journey to becoming a learning-game designer is to play some learning games. You will get the chance to see how core dynamics, game mechanics, and game elements are used to influence the learning experience and provide an engaging game-play experience.

Exploring Learning Games

In This Chapter

✓ What is a learning game?
✓ Are games effective tools for learning?
✓ What is the difference between learning games and entertainment games?
✓ Sample evaluation: Zombie Sales Apocalypse
✓ Work on your own

Now that you have played and evaluated some entertainment games, it's time to explore learning games and how they differ from those designed purely for entertainment and fun. Figure 3-1 shows you where we are in the learning-game design process.

Figure 3-1. Learning-Game Design Process: Explore Learning Games

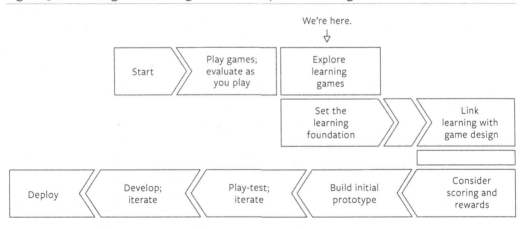

What Is a Learning Game?

In the learning and development field, there are several types of interactive learning experiences that often get confused with one another. As someone who will be designing a learning game, you need to know the difference between learning games, simulations, and gamification, as well as the differences between entertainment games and games designed for a learning outcome.

When you discuss your plans to create a learning game, everyone involved in the design, development, and implementation of the game needs to understand exactly what is being developed. If you don't discuss definitions beforehand, miscommunication and divergent expectations may result.

Share the following definitions with stakeholders when you discuss the design and creation of your learning game. Doing so eliminates confusion and clarifies if a learning game is the right solution or if a different approach, such as a simulation or the use of gamification, is more appropriate.

- **Entertainment games,** the focus of chapter 2, are purely for enjoyment. There is no other expected outcome. Most people are familiar with entertainment games because they have played them. Players may learn from an entertainment game, but learning is not the goal. If any learning occurs, it is a by-product or incidental to the goal of enjoyment.

- **Learning games** are designed to help players develop new knowledge or skills or to reinforce existing knowledge or skills. Learning games are also called "serious games" or "instructional games." The end goal of a learning game is to achieve some type of learning outcome while being engaged or immersed in the learning process. Learning games often rely on an abstraction of reality and an element of fantasy in the teaching process, and often are not an exact replica of a real-life situation. The fun within the game should link to what's being learned as much as possible.

- **Simulations** are an attempt to reproduce reality. They are an interactive experience that provides learners with a realistic, controlled-risk environment to practice specific behaviors and experience the effects of their decisions. A famous example of a learning simulation is the flight simulator that airlines and NASA use to train pilots. The lines between simulations and learning games are often blurred because simulations may include points, competition between players, and even high scores. The main difference to keep in mind is the importance of reality and how closely the designer mirrors what happens within the simulation to real life.

- **Gamification** is the use of game elements in a learning situation, but not the creation of an entire game. It is using parts of the game in the design of instruction, as opposed to creating an entire game. A common example is to award points for learners to accomplish a certain task and then create a leaderboard and have learners compete to earn the highest score. The activities are not part of a game but have points assigned to them. Earning a badge after learning about a compliance rule would be another example. To learn more about gamification, see Karl's books *The Gamification of Learning and Instruction* and *The Gamification of Learning and Instruction Fieldbook.*

These interactive learning tools can all be effective for reaching a desired learning outcome, but each has a different purpose and focus. Simulations are best when you want a realistic, high-fidelity experience for the learner. Gamification is effective when you want the learners to be engaged with content or an experience over a long period. Gamification is also good for reinforcing content and information previously covered in a workshop or webinar. Learning games are effective when you want to immerse the player in the content and experience and provide an abstract experience to teach concepts or ideas.

Remember that simulations, gamification, and learning games can all be created in either online or face-to-face formats. Often people think that learning games or simulations need to be online, but that is not the case, or even the best approach. In many corporate environments, board games or card games are effective ways to reinforce knowledge and concepts. It's also not uncommon to use badges or points in a classroom to motivate learners. When designing a learning game, keep your options open. Often a simple card game can be a cost-effective way to achieve a desired learning outcome.

Are Games Effective for Learning?

We are often asked whether learning games actually facilitate learning. The short answer is yes. Evidence strongly supports the conclusion that games are capable of being effective, efficient tools for teaching—players of instructional games can and do learn from games.

Several meta-analyses (studies of studies) have indicated that game-based learning is more effective for learning than traditional classroom instruction. In fact, Pieter Wouters and colleagues (2013) compared results from 38 individual studies and found that learning games or serious games more effectively promote learning and retention than conventional methods. They also found that learners in serious games learned more, relative to those taught with conventional instruction methods (lectures and discussions), when the game was augmented with other instructional methods, when multiple training sessions were involved, and when players worked in groups.

Traci Sitzmann (2011) conducted a meta-analysis of 65 independent samples and data from more than 6,000 trainees and found that trainees who had played games as opposed to participating in conventional instructional methods "had 11% higher declarative knowledge levels, 14% higher procedural knowledge levels, and 9% higher retention levels than trainees in the comparison group." She also found that the games were "17% more effective than lecture and 5% more effective than discussion, the two most popular instructional methods in classroom instruction."

In another study, Thomas M. Connolly and colleagues (2012) conducted a meta-analysis by reviewing 129 papers reporting evidence related to the outcomes of computer games and serious games with respect to learning and engagement. One strong conclusion they reached was that the most "frequently occurring outcomes and impacts were knowledge acquisition/content understanding and affective and motivational outcomes." It's clear that learning games are a highly proficient form of instruction for obtaining desired learning results.

However, games—like any other instructional solution—need to be carefully designed, developed, and implemented to facilitate learning. Poorly designed games, like poorly designed classroom instruction, yield poor learning outcomes. When you design a learning game, you need to know the game features and elements that lead to learning and include them in your design.

Learning Games Versus Entertainment Games

Creating a learning game is not an easy process; there are many elements required for a learning game that are not normally included in an entertainment game. Additionally, because the focus is on learning, the design process centers on elements that foster learning, but still relies on common game elements to make the experience worthwhile and motivating for the learner.

Game Goals Versus Instructional Goals

Every learning game needs to have a game goal and an instructional goal (Table 3-1). The game goal is what the player does to win the game. It might be finding the treasure, capturing a ship, earning the most money, or acquiring the most territory. The instructional goal is what the player is expected to learn. It might be something like learning how to fix a leaky faucet, identify an adverse medical event, deal with an angry customer, or comply with government regulations.

Identifying both the instructional goal and the game goal is important from an overall design perspective. When you're designing a learning game, the instructional goal must take precedent. If the players don't learn from your game, it's not a learning game, no matter how much fun they have playing.

Table 3-1. Examples of Game and Instructional Goals

Game Name	Game Goal	Instructional Goal
Quest	Acquire the most territory.	As an account manager, communicate the right product value propositions to customers using stories.
Power of Protection	Be the first one to make it to the corner office.	Ensure members' protected health information stays secure according to HIPPA privacy standards.
Searching for Fraud	Find the hidden treasure.	As a health insurance provider, prevent and detect fraud, waste, and abuse in your work environment.
Moon Landing	Be the first one to land on the moon.	Follow the key requirements of the Sarbanes-Oxley Act that apply to your position as an external auditor.

Note that at this point in the process, we are creating instructional goals and not measurable learning objectives. Later in the design process you will need to break down the instructional goal into measurable learning objectives.

Less Is Better

The phrase *less is better* has several applications when designing a learning game. The first mistake many new learning-game designers make is trying to teach everything in the game. They'll take the entire sales process and try to make it into a game, from prospecting the potential client to making additional sales. Or they'll take all the rules and regulations regarding compliance and stuff them into a single game. The best rule to follow when you create a learning game is to start small. For example, perhaps you design a game to teach the prospecting process and save the rest of the sales process for later. A learning game can quickly become too big or too complicated to fit the timeframe in which you want to use it. It is best to start with a specific instructional goal and expand later if the learning need requires it.

Additionally, strive to keep rules simple. In entertainment games, people often willingly spend time learning the rules so they can use them to their advantage, and they don't mind some ramp-up time for understanding the game and game play. This is not the case for learning games, so you want the rules to be simple and easy to understand. Carefully balance the complexity of your game mechanics and elements with the learning needs of the game. You don't want the players to spend valuable time figuring out the game. Rules that are too cumbersome can lead to cognitive overload, and players will be learning only how to play the game and not the desired instructional goal. Game play that is too complex will frustrate learners and distract them from the learning they need to do.

However, it's a good idea to build triggers into the game to provide guidance if learners suddenly encounter some difficulty. Instructional prompts, tips, and hints need to be included within the learning game.

Finally, consider how long your game takes to play; you don't want to create an epic 14-hour game. In typical corporate environments, players have limited time to play and multiple distractions competing for their attention. Keep the timeframe relatively short and focused. If the game takes too long to play, learners will quickly abandon it and view it as a waste of time.

Don't Focus on Entertainment

Learning games need to be what we call "fun enough." Many new learning-game developers try to design an entertaining game. Unfortunately, that often makes learning harder rather than easier. Remember, you are not creating the next great commercial game to entertain your learners; you are creating a learning game in which success will be measured by the achievement of learning outcomes.

Resist the temptation to create a ton of rules, pile on different game elements, and incorporate multiple dynamics to keep player interest high. Yes, the game should be engaging with a mild level of fun, but learning should be the goal. Focus on engagement rather than entertainment. The goals of the game play should be interactivity and engagement. Research shows that what makes games instructional is the level of interactivity and engagement the learners have with the content (Sitzmann 2011). Given those parameters, making sure the learners are engaged and active is far more important than making sure they are entertained.

Include as Part of a Larger Learning Design

Commercial games such as Angry Birds, *Assassin's Creed*, or Monopoly are usually played without context: A group of friends simply start playing a game, either online or in person. However, for a learning game to be the most effective, it needs to be part of a larger instructional plan and include instructional support elements. You can't simply create a game and expect the players to learn from it without providing any context or guidance. For learning games to work, they need to be an integral part of a larger learning design.

The best learning-game outcomes occur when a three-step embedding process is followed. First, an instructor or online directions introduce the game and explain its learning objectives to the players. Second, the players play the game. Third, after the game is played, the instructor and players should debrief about what was learned and how the game's events support the instructional objectives. If an instructor is not available, such as for an online game, provide the players with questions to prompt them to think about what they learned in the game. This process helps ensure that learning occurs as a result of playing the game (Hays 2005; Sitzmann 2011).

Don't Focus on Winning

Sometimes learners can become engrossed in winning the game while failing to focus on learning. They get distracted by collecting resources, competing against time constraints, or accumulating points. The learning outcome gets overshadowed by rule complexity or too many game elements. To avoid this problem, you need to focus on two design principles.

The first principle is that winning must be contingent on learning. You can't design a learning game in which a player could win because of luck or chance. Create the game so that winning is directly related to acquiring or demonstrating knowledge. An example of this is Trivial Pursuit. In the game, the color a player lands on is determined by a roll of the dice. However, to win the game, players must correctly answer a question in every category and complete their pie. Chance plays a role, but knowledge is key to winning.

The second principle is that both a losing state and a winning state need to lead to learning. You need to design the game play to encourage learning throughout the game, and consider what happens when a player is not successful. If you create a competitive game, remember that there will be winners and losers, and sometimes the losers will feel bad and get upset. So, winning should not be overemphasized. Work to incorporate learning into all aspects of the game so that all players have learned the key information, regardless of their standing when the game is finished.

Keep in mind that players who do not win at the learning game may get angry at the instructor, other players, or the game itself; get frustrated at their lack of progress or ability to win; or try to cheat or game the system to gain an advantage. They may be temporarily saddened by the entire learning experience or visibly upset. They may feel incompetent and wonder why they can't win. They may even feel isolated because everyone else seems to be winning and having a good time and they are losing.

When you decide to create a learning game with winners and losers, you need to find a way to deal with those who do not win. You need to help them avoid some of these negative feelings. You may even decide that a cooperative game is better.

Here are some tips to help mitigate losing in a learning or serious game:

- Forewarn players that they might become upset or frustrated if they find themselves losing, but that is part of the learning process.
- Inform players that they might lose the game and that is OK, because learning will still occur.
- Carefully brief all players on the instructional objectives of the game and de-emphasize winning.
- Acknowledge the frustration or anger at losing.
- Ask players to find lessons within the loss. Have them analyze why they lost and ask, "Can those insights lead to learning?"
- Don't spend too much time extolling the winners. Acknowledge them and move right to the instructional lesson.
- Provide a list of strategies that will help the players win next time.
- Within the curriculum, follow the game activity with an activity in which everyone can feel positive.
- If players are in a classroom, allow those who did not win a chance to discuss why they didn't. If they're online, provide chat opportunities.
- Consider whether creating a win-loss situation is what you want in the learning experience. Sometimes it is appropriate, but be prepared for unintended consequences and negative feedback if you don't handle the situation properly.
- Create different levels of winning: Players can win a round or one task, or they can experience small victories throughout the game. This is helpful because if players fall behind early, they may mentally drop out early in the learning process. Find ways to keep them engaged.
- Consider building a cooperative rather than a competitive game. Working together is far more inclusive than competition.

Evaluate a Learning Game

Remember that learning games can be simple or more complex. Here is a game called Zombie Sales Apocalypse, which is designed to teach sales skills to players. The game takes place in a medical office building, where players are attempting to sell a cure (and their product) to a doctor. It can be found at www.zombiesalesgame.com. Let's walk through it (Table 3-2). You can then evaluate a learning game on your own.

Table 3-2. Zombie Sales Apocalypse

What Is the Game Goal?
The goal of the game is to avoid the zombies and sell an antidote to the doctors. For some people, running from zombies, blasting through walls, and using furniture as a blockade is engaging. It can also be engaging when a nonplayer character has turned into a zombie and keeps pushing the player. It adds tension as well.

What Is the Instructional Goal?
The instructional goal is to learn how to apply the sales model properly to make a sale to an entire doctor's office. This includes knowing what to say to the receptionist, nurses, and doctor. The game is designed to reinforce the model by providing feedback to players about how well they applied the sales model in the situation.

What Core Dynamics Were Used?
The core dynamic is to escape from the zombies by properly applying the elements of the sales model and answering the branching questions. The game is a branching adventure game in which you must choose the right branch to be successful.

List at Least 3 Game Mechanics From the Game
Explicit game mechanics include avoid zombies, click on nonplayer characters to engage in conversation, collect documents before they are needed in the conversation, collect boosts used to avoid zombies and smash through walls, and click on furniture and drag to impede zombie progress. Behind the scenes, mechanics exist to indicate to the nonplayer character, Dirk, where to run after a conversation and what to do in a particular room.

Identify and Describe Game Elements Used in the Game		
Aesthetics Story Chance **Conflict** **Competition** Cooperation	Levels Resources **Rewards** Strategy **Theme** Time	One element is theme. The game is based on the idea that people are infected with a zombie virus, and players have to sell their products to introduce the antidote. Another element is conflict. Players are in conflict with zombies, who are trying to zap their strength. The game provides rewards in the form of the yellow "boosts," which can be used to blast through walls or freeze zombies. The aesthetic of the game is a dark, horror-genre atmosphere. The game provides competition with a leaderboard, where players can compare their progress with others.

What Feedback Did You Get for How You Were Doing?

Players have several cues that provide information on progress. One is that if they do something wrong, a zombie appears. They also can see the progress they are making on each element of the sales model on a meter that is being completed.

Other Notes

The game used an engaging scenario and allowed you to apply sales training in an effective way.

The process of breaking down a game doesn't need to be lengthy or involve a great deal of complexity. And, by analyzing various learning games, you will begin to understand how the game conventions and elements of learning games differ from entertainment games. You will also start forming judgments about what makes an effective or ineffective learning game.

Work on Your Own

Now that we've gone over the process of breaking down a learning game, here's a simple one for you to try doing on your own.

Password Blaster (Figure 3-2) is a simple game that will give you an idea of the difference between a learning game and an entertainment game. It is designed to help learners distinguish between a weak password and a strong password. As you play, you need to remember that you are playing this game outside of its original context. This game is a small piece of a larger curriculum on information asset protection. The overarching curriculum goal is to get employees to follow best practices in keeping company data and equipment secure. The employees had already participated in other learning activities and had access to an online e-magazine on information asset protection. The game reinforced the idea of creating strong passwords.

Figure 3-2. Password Blaster

For this exercise, you will only play the game; you won't see the other curriculum elements. You will then evaluate it to determine the differences between entertainment and learning games.

Access the game at www.bottomlineperformance.com/passwordblaster or download it to your smartphone from either Google Play or the App Store by searching "Bottom-Line Performance Password Blaster." Spend about five minutes playing, and then fill out the worksheet found in appendix 3 or at www.td.org/PlaytoLearnExtras. The answer key is in appendix 4.

Want to Play More Learning Games?

It can be tough to find learning games to play and evaluate. Here are a few websites you can check out. Many of the games are for K-12 rather than adult learners, but they still provide great sources of ideas.

iCivics (www.icivics.org/games) was founded by Justice Sandra Day O'Connor and is designed to invigorate civic learning through interactive and engaging learning activities. Playing the learning games can give you a sense of how game play is mixed with learning about civics.

Nobelprize.org (www.nobelprize.org/educational) has many games based on Nobel Prize–winning work. While the games are aimed more at young children, the mixture of educational focus and game play can be informative for anyone thinking of designing a learning game.

Games for Change (www.gamesforchange.org/play) has a great variety of games focused on helping bring about social change. Some games are targeted to kids, but many others are for all ages.

Wrap-Up

Learning games are an effective method of instruction, but they need to focus on a particular outcome. Additionally, the idea of "entertainment" is a secondary consideration to learning when you're creating learning games. In the next chapter, we will discuss linking the goals of a learning game directly to a business need, developing player personas, and creating an instructional design checklist for the development of your learning games.

Part 2

Making Game Design Choices That Support Learning

Setting the Right Foundation for Your Learning Game

In This Chapter

✓ Why do you define the business need for a learning game?
✓ What is an instructional goal?
✓ What are player personas?
✓ Defining constraints
✓ Defining learning objectives
✓ Putting it all together: Instructional design checklist
✓ Work on your own

We're moving right along in our learning-game design process. This chapter focuses on creating the instructional design foundation for your game (Figure 4-1).

Figure 4-1. The Learning-Game Design Process: Set the Learning Foundation

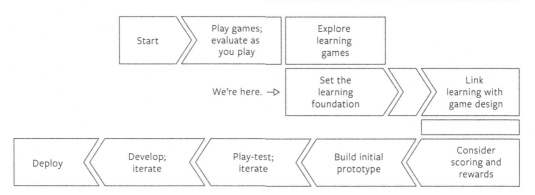

Defining the Business Need

You've likely heard this advice before: Clarify the problem you need to solve before you start designing anything, and agree on how success can be measured. Before you jump into creating a learning game, make sure you understand what problem the business hopes to solve and how you will assess whether it has been solved. Then make sure you create an instructional goal and that the learning objectives clearly align with solving this business problem. If you are going to ask employees to play a game, the game needs to link to learning and help accelerate performance.

Let's start with the business needs a company might have that training can help address. A business need, if met, will produce a quantifiable change. Table 4-1 lists three examples of business needs and quantifiable evidence of change based on projects we've done in the past.

Table 4-1. Examples of Business Need

Business Need or Problem	Quantifiable Goal or Evidence of Success	Impact on Business
Ramp-up time for new hires needs to be reduced. It currently takes almost 12 months to reach full proficiency in the role.	Reduction in ramp-up time; ability to handle most common tasks associated with role without assistance within six months of hire.	• Increased revenue generated by fully productive employees. • Decreased costs associated with onboarding time.
Employee turnover is higher than the industry average. It is stressing daily operations inside restaurants, adversely affecting customer satisfaction ratings, and reducing profitability.	Decrease in annual turnover from 300 to 250 percent, a 17 percent reduction.	• Improved customer satisfaction scores. • Decreased recruiting and hiring costs. • Increased revenue per store. • Lower manager-level turnover due to burnout and stress of constant hiring and training.
Training time required to train new customers on a hospital laboratory testing unit is too long and customer-help needs persist for months.	Decrease on-site training time requirements from four weeks to five days; decrease customer support calls by at least 10 percent.	• Expanded bandwidth of existing technical trainers so they can support more customers. • Reduced customer support costs.

You can design learning games that help solve all these business problems—but only if you first know what problem you need to solve. Without clear direction on what problem you are trying to address and what measure you need to hit, you can create fun games that provide no real value to the organization.

You would think stakeholders and subject matter experts (SMEs) could quickly and easily tell you what business problem they want to solve. Sometimes, though, asking a SME or stakeholder, "What is the problem and how can you quantify it?" leads to "I don't know." However, you don't have to accept that initial response.

Here's an example of how you might proceed. Let's say the first thing the SME says to you is, "We don't have any actual numbers, but I've been hearing from the field that this is an issue. I've talked to our lab chemists and they tell me that they are answering the same questions over and over. They are sharing basic information that field reps should really know themselves. If they were able to answer questions, I know it would be beneficial to our company."

The SME may very well be right, but you should still gather more information. If this is really a big issue that costs the company money, chances are the data are not as difficult to assemble as the SME thinks. To help quantify this issue and its impact on the company, you can ask, "How many chemists are affected by a sales rep's need to call for technical support?"

You can then talk to the chemists. Ask them, "In a given week, how many calls or emails from sales reps do you respond to and what are the most common issues? How much time do you spend on this per week—30 minutes, an hour, two hours?"

You can also ask the distributors to give you insights. Ask a handful of them these kinds of questions:

- How frequently do you ask a sales rep a product question that she cannot answer?
- If a rep cannot answer you immediately, can you quantify any dollar impact to your business?
- How does your expectations regarding a rep's ability to answer your questions affect your perception of ACME as a supplier?

Another technique you can use is to ask the stakeholder to give you a dollar value that he would associate with whatever problem he describes to you: Is it worth $10,000, $20,000, or $30,000? Why? What benefit will ACME get by solving this problem? Sometimes, the act of asking stakeholders or SMEs to assign a dollar value can help them realize they need more data before jumping to solution design. After all, the data might help create a better solution!

If it is worth $10,000 or less, you are not looking at a very robust learning solution. And if you are not looking at a robust solution, will you truly affect performance change? Even if a solution is designed, developed, and delivered entirely internally, the cost is likely to quickly approach at least $10,000 when you factor in the time for a designer to design and build the program, a SME to provide content expertise, and employees to complete the training program.

Defining Your Instructional Goal

Once you know what business problem you need to help resolve—and you have a clear operational target—you can formulate your instructional goals for your training solution, which frequently will consist of more than a single learning game. As chapter 3 discussed, it's better to embed a game within a curriculum than use a game by itself to address all learning objectives. You may use several learning tools to achieve the instructional goal; games may be one of the tools, but shouldn't be the only one you use.

Your instructional goal should describe the desired end state of learner performance. It should support the business goal and be verifiable. You then use learning objectives to define everything learners need to know to achieve the instructional goal.

Table 4-2 presents examples of three business needs and the associated instructional goals for training programs we developed to help meet the need. Each of the training programs included one or more games as methods for helping achieve the instructional goal.

Table 4-2. Business Needs and Related Instructional Goals

Business Need	Instructional Goal
Increase the number of parts sold per customer.	After playing this game, sales reps will have an expanded perception of the kinds of customers to whom they can sell. They can link relevant product families to a variety of applications and technologies within specific customer types.
Decrease time to productivity for new hires.	At the end of the first year, new associates can complete research and fieldwork independently, perform the major tasks of a given engagement, and perform administrative procedures required within their service group. (Note: This goal spanned an entire curriculum; a game was one solution used within the curriculum.)
Better equip sales reps to sell new products.	Account managers will be able to fluently communicate the right product value propositions to customers using stories.

After you agree on an instructional goal, you need to get a clear picture of the learners you want to reach with your game. This includes crafting a player persona (or perhaps multiple personas if you expect different audiences to play the game) as your next step.

Crafting Player Personas

Most learning and development professionals are familiar with the term *audience analysis*. To maximize the effectiveness of your learning game, you need to analyze your audience. By crafting a player persona, you can go beyond a typical audience analysis and paint a vivid picture of who will play your game. This means gathering more than simple demographic data; ideally, you will interact with the target learners. If that is not possible, make sure someone on your design team has firsthand knowledge of the target: Either she has been in the learners' role in the past or the learners report to her.

Marketing professionals have long used buyer personas to gain a clear picture of whom they are selling to, what motivates them, and what strategies work best to target them. They base the personas on real market-research data, but fictionalize them to a degree to describe a single buyer, which personalizes the buyer for the marketer.

Your player personas should be similar. Base your personas on the research you do to help you understand their goals, motivations, challenges, and daily work flows. Add to these any company data that exist on age, gender, educational background, years of experience, and so on. Table 4-3 offers an example of a tool you can use to help create a persona. The column on the left identifies the type of information you want to gather and questions you want to answer. The column on the right is an example that shows you the right level of information detail to gather.

Table 4-3. Information-Gathering Tool for Player Persona

Persona Element and Description	Example
Name: Give your persona a name. You want this persona to feel real to you and not be a bunch of statistics.	Cheryl
Demographics (age, gender, ethnicity, college, etc.): Make your training look like your learner. Don't assume anything.	Age 41, Caucasian, female. Four-year degree from a small liberal arts college. Majored in communications, achieved numerous academic honors.
Experience with the company, within the role: What is representational of your learner? Go with the median, not the average. Averages can fool you.	Ten years' experience in pharmaceutical sales with specific experience in three therapeutic areas: cardiovascular, primary care, and gastroenterology. Shifted to selling biologics three years ago.
Biggest challenges on the job: Most roles have common challenges; find them and include them in your persona.	• Pace—the days are long • Keeping up—there's always more she could read to stay abreast of trends, issues, and competitors
What does she value most about the role? What motivates this person regarding the role? What makes her want to do this particular job? Your training can acknowledge both challenges and values.	• Being credible • Knowing her product helps patients have a better quality of life • Hitting goals she sets for herself

Table 4-3. Information-Gathering Tool for Player Persona

Persona Element and Description	Example
Workday flow: How does a day go from start to finish? Your training should reflect understanding of the workday flow.	• Because her territory is urban, Cheryl may schedule as many as eight appointments in a day. • She's up at 6 a.m., with her kids getting up at 6:30. She starts her "work" day around 7:30 and often ends as late as 10 p.m., although she may take a break in the late afternoon. • Evenings vary. If there is a professional meeting, she could be dining with healthcare providers (HCPs) at that meeting. If there's no meeting, she could be planning calls for the next day, entering notes into Salesforce, catching up on reading, or responding to emails.
Sales call flow: Be clear on how the rep sells the product you are helping her learn about. Learn how much time a good sales call takes. Map what you believe reps need to know and know how to do with what they will actually use in a sales call. **Types of calls made in a typical day:** Find out how many types of sales calls there are. If there are several different call types, make sure your training program reflects this reality.	• Calls need to follow a "ladder" process. Early calls have different sales call objectives than later sales calls. Each "rung" of the ladder has a specific call objective and message associated with it. • Call lengths vary from five minutes to 20 minutes. • Early calls educate HCPs on the product category. Later calls provide information on specific products. • There are two categories of customers: clinicians and pharmacy. • Getting from the bottom of the ladder to the top may take anywhere from six weeks to a few months.
Devices and how they are used during the flow of a day: Design for the device that reps use the most.	• Uses laptop in early mornings and late evenings. Does planning activities; documents information in Salesforce; takes e-learning courses (because they're not available for phone or tablet). • Phone is constantly in her hand throughout her day. She uses it to track appointments, check and respond to emails and voice messages, and put quick notes into Salesforce between calls. • Uses tablet to pull sales aids up on tablet when talking with HCPs, if needed and appropriate.
Where self-paced training will be completed: Setting matters because it tells you how distracted reps are likely to be, how much time is realistic to allocate for any self-paced segments, and whether sound is a good or bad option to include.	• Wherever she can squeeze it in. Usually she's at home, later in the evening while she sips some herbal tea or has a glass of wine. She may also start her day with it, leaving it to a Friday when she does more home office work. • If she had access through a phone, she could do small bits between sales calls or while grabbing some lunch.

Persona Element and Description	Example
Games played and amount of time spent playing them: Ask your targets what games they play, how much time they spend playing them, and how frequently they play.	• Cheryl is slightly embarrassed to admit it, but she is completely addicted to Candy Crush and other simple mobile games like it. It's almost a stress reliever for her. She'll play it whenever she's in line. • She also likes playing board games with her kids.

Once you gather the information in table form, your next step is to convert this into a more concise format useful to your team. Often personas are shown to a team as presentation slides or printed so they can be posted on a workroom wall for ongoing reference throughout design and development of the learning solution. Figure 4-2 shows an example of this repackaging into a more concise persona. We used Sharon's picture here to provide an example image for inclusion in the persona summary. When you create your personas, search for images that capture their essence and help you think of the real players represented by the personas.

Figure 4-2. Example of a Learning Persona Created for a Game

"Show me how to use info within a sales call. Keep it simple. Make it easy to access and use."

Challenges
- Getting it all done in a day
- Keeping up with the new stuff

Values
- Knowing her product helps patients feel better
- Being a credible voice to healthcare providers
- Hitting her goals

- **Personal Profile**
  Cheryl is 41; she has two kids and is constantly on the go, between her job and her kids' activities. Cheryl has been with Axis Pharma for 10 years, all of them as a sales rep. She's a seasoned pro and proud of her skills as a rep.

- **Sales Call Flow**
  There is a "ladder approach" to selling her product. The first two to three calls focus on the product category; the second two to three calls focus on the product itself. There is a specific call objective and message for each type of call. Getting up the ladder in a new account takes weeks to months. Call durations vary from five to 20 minutes, depending on the objective and the healthcare provider's availability.

- **A Day in Her Life**
  Days are long. Cheryl's up at 6 a.m. The workday starts at 7:30; it may end around 10 p.m., when she wraps up a dinner meeting, emails, or inputting notes into Salesforce. Her territory is urban; she can make up to eight calls in a day.

- **Devices and Gaming**
  Cheryl starts and ends the day with her laptop. Her phone is her go-to device during the day for email, voicemail, and Internet searches. She uses her tablet mostly during sales calls. Cheryl enjoys quick mobile games that can be used as "time fillers." She and her family also enjoy an occasional board or card game that is easy to learn and play. They enjoy spending about an hour or two playing together, which is probably about once a month.

Defining Constraints

Every project has constraints. Every game you create should consider constraints from your players or the play environment, such as the following:

- **Amount of time.** This is the time you can reasonably expect players to focus on your game amid their job duties and its pressures. The amount of time available affects the scope and complexity of your game, and the content you include.

- **Location where players might play your game.** Are players going to be playing in a noisy environment? The degree of distractions a player might have definitely has an impact on complexity. It can also affect the use of sound.

- **Device most frequently available to players.** For digital games, you want to avoid designing to a laptop device if the device that players will have access to most frequently is their phone.

- **Technical constraints posed by your organization.** For example, does the game need to pass data to your learning management system? Does it need to run on both Android and iOS? Are downloads required? Get your IT team involved earlier rather than later if you are planning to create a digital game.

- **Development time constraints.** How much time do you have to develop the game? If you have two weeks, you are not developing the same type of game that you would if you had six months.

- **Resource constraints.** The skills and abilities of your team influence the kind of game you can create. The amount of money you have to spend also affects what you can do.

- **Attitudes and experiences of your target players.** There is no point in developing an immersive, multiplayer online experience for a target group of players who are completely unfamiliar with the genre. Stick with games that will resonate with your target.

In the player persona shown in Figure 4-2, the information leads to these possible conclusions:

- Players' time will be extremely limited and in short segments of availability. Any self-paced, online game play needs to be kept short.

- Game play should be simple. The game will be played in shorter bursts; therefore, it needs to have simple rules that are easy for players to learn and remember.

- Game content should focus on selling environments and scenarios, rather than simple recall. This will make the game most meaningful to target players and keep them motivated to play.

- Points and rewards need to appeal to players' goal-orientation. Money as a scoring mechanism may appeal, as will percentages of territory acquired or customer satisfaction ratings that increase or decrease based on player decisions.

- Game content should reflect the call ladder reps must climb to close a sale.
- Because reps are primarily using a phone, a game that is playable on a phone as opposed to a laptop might be better.
- This audience is middle-aged; the text should be very readable, even on older phones.
- In the live environment, board games will work well.

Defining Learning Objectives

You have a clear business problem, a related instructional goal, and a clear picture of your players. Your next step is to define your learning objectives. Learning objectives should help you answer this question: To achieve this instructional goal, what do my learners need to:

- know
- know how to do
- believe or feel?

Use Bloom's Taxonomy to help you craft your objectives and accurately assess what level of cognitive skill learners need to achieve your goal. Be aware that these levels don't function in isolation of one another. Most tasks require multiple levels of cognition to be used simultaneously. However, Bloom's provides a reasonable way of organizing the learning experience so learners can build skills in steps. It categorizes learning into six levels of thinking, with each level adding complexity. The original taxonomy is from 1956, with a revised taxonomy developed in 2001. The revised version flips the final two levels and uses different synonyms to describe the lowest level of cognition.

Your task as the learning-game designer is to choose a game type that enables the player to achieve the cognitive skill required. Most of all, make sure your learning objectives map to your instructional goal, and your game type enables players to achieve the objectives.

Once you know the skill level you want players to achieve, you can choose a game type that can help them achieve targeted skills. Table 4-4 summarizes the original taxonomy and offers suggestions on game types appropriate for each level. The left column defines the cognitive skill. The middle column lists examples of behaviors you might include in a learning objective that targets that level. The right column identifies game types that work well for that level. The list is not comprehensive; it merely provides starting ideas.

You'll also see that some game types can work for multiple levels. In addition, the content within your game can dictate what level of cognitive skill is required to play it successfully. A quiz-style game can focus primarily on recall, or it can require higher-level skills in analysis, synthesis, or evaluation, depending on how you structure the question and what content you include.

Table 4-4. Bloom's Taxonomy and Game Types

Cognitive Skill	Sample Verbs for Learning Objectives at This Level (Barton 1997)	Game Types to Consider
Level 1: Knowledge Know and remember facts or ideas.	List, identify, recognize, name, match, select, recite	Quiz-style, arcade-style, matching, game-show styles
Level 2: Comprehension Understand the facts or ideas; be able to explain them accurately.	Explain, describe, compare, contrast, distinguish, summarize, rephrase, tell	Quiz-style, collection and classification games, exploration games, storytelling games
Level 3: Application Use facts or ideas to solve problems or respond to situations.	Use, demonstrate, choose, solve, organize, develop, build, make use of	Story- or scenario-based quiz games, matching games, role-playing games, decision games involving scenarios, simulations
Level 4: Analysis Break information into parts and identify causes; make inferences and form generalizations based on examination of facts.	Analyze, compare, infer, categorize, classify, distinguish, conclude, describe relationships	Strategy games
Level 5: Synthesis Organize and combine information to form alternative solutions.	Compile, create, estimate, invent, choose, design, predict, combine, develop	Building games, simulations
Level 6: Evaluation Judge information and facts against a set of criteria. Form opinions and ideas based on this judgment and be able to defend them.	Determine, critique, decide, prioritize, assess, evaluate, deduce, justify	Simulations, role-playing games

Here's an example of an instructional goal and associated learning objectives. The instructional goal targets Level 3 skills (application), but to be effective the sales rep may also need to use some Level 4 skills (analysis). We identified each objective's skill level. You might create games for one, some, or all of the objectives.

Instructional Goal: Account managers can communicate the right product value propositions to customers using stories. The learning objectives learners need to master to achieve the goal include:

- Select the appropriate tools to support the system. (Level 1)
- Explain the features, associated benefits, and stories. (Level 2)
- Given a customer need, choose the right features and articulate the associated benefit. (Level 3)
- Ask the right questions to uncover the customer's needs. (Level 3)
- Tailor the value proposition and stories to the customer's needs. (Level 3)
- Contrast the [product name] methods with other methods of the past. (Level 4)
- Given a real customer, put together an appropriate story. (Level 5)
- Overcome customer objections. (Level 6)

Simple Games Can Lead to Complex Thinking

Don't assume that remaining at a lower level means the thinking required is simple or not valuable. A game designed to enable comprehension can be quite powerful and spark change. In her TED Talk "Games for a Change," game designer Brenda Brathwaite (2012) described a deceptively simple game she created for her 7-year-old daughter. She shared that her daughter was studying the Middle Passage in school; she could recite facts about this historical journey, but she clearly did not understand the meaning behind them. So Brathwaite used an index card as a boat and game pieces to represent African family members captured by slave traders. Her daughter painted them various colors, with each color representing a family. She and her daughter filled the boat with people. The game had four rules:

- The game has 10 turns.
- You have 30 units of food.
- On each turn, roll the die.
- Use that amount of food.

As her daughter rolled the die, it became clear there would not be enough food to last the journey. People were going to die. Brathwaite's daughter realized that the Middle Passage was more than facts. She saw that family members got separated and that this was not a journey anyone would want to take. The game helped her daughter convert facts to understanding.

Instructional Design Checklist

Table 4-5 compiles everything discussed in this chapter into a format you can use to start documenting your game's instructional design. The questions within it are not exhaustive, but will help you get started. The next chapter will add questions focused on game design and how you link game design decisions to your instructional goal, player personas, learning objectives, and constraints.

Table 4-5. Learning Games Checklist: Part 1: Instructional Design Questions

Business Need

- What's the business need that's driving the use of a learning game?
  - ☐ A need to increase sales or support the launch of a new product?
  - ☐ Customer complaints or ineffective customer service?
  - ☐ A need to comply with government regulations?
  - ☐ Quality issues?
  - ☐ Safety issues?
- What measures would offer evidence that the game was helpful in resolving the business need?
  - ☐ Decreased costs?
  - ☐ Decreased employee ramp-up?
  - ☐ Greater productivity?
  - ☐ Greater revenue?
  - ☐ Greater profit margins?
  - ☐ Other?

Instructional Goal

- What will players be doing on the job if they learn from the game?
- What behavior can eliminate the business problem or solve the business need?

Learning Objectives

- What do players need to know to achieve the instructional goal?
- What do they need to know how to do?
- What do they need to believe or feel?
- What common mistakes are they likely to make and do we want them to avoid?

Player Persona

- Representative name
- Key demographic info and relevant experience
- Need statement
- Biggest challenges
- Motivators and values
- Workflow and workday realities
- Devices used
- Game play experience and expectations

Constraints to Consider

- Technology (devices, operating systems, LMS issues, IT and security)
- Time constraints (development side and player side)
- Resources and expertise available to produce and support game

Work on Your Own

Appendix 5 offers a blank worksheet that can form the beginning of your game design document. Use it to document the instructional design for a game you hope to create. As needed, refer to the explanations and examples in this chapter to produce a summary of your game's instructional design. Note that your game design document may summarize information from the detailed player persona you create rather than including all the detail you put into it.

Wrap-Up

Good instructional design is the foundation of a good learning game. Make sure you understand what problem you are trying to solve, how you will measure whether you succeed, and what instructional goal and objectives lead you to solving it. Finally, be sure you have a clear picture of your player and of any constraints you must factor in as you begin designing your solution.

Linking Learning With Game Design

In This Chapter

✓ How do instructional goals factor into game design?
✓ Why do you need to match core dynamics and game mechanics to learning needs?
✓ How do you choose game elements that support learning?
✓ Work on your own

We're ready to start thinking about the game design (Figure 5-1). This chapter covers goals, rules, and game elements.

Figure 5-1. The Learning-Game Design Process: Link Learning With Game Design

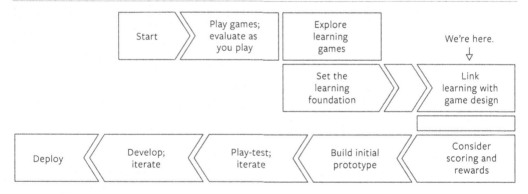

In chapter 4, you identified the learning foundation you need to create before you start designing a game. This chapter digs into the specifics of game design: game goals, game mechanics, and game elements. Thinking through the decisions related to these components will help you balance the need to keep learners engaged with the need for people to learn.

The Instructional Goal as a Springboard to a Game Design

Chapter 3 introduced you to instructional goals as a distinct element of learning games. The instructional goal and associated learning objectives are the springboard for your learning game's design conversation. This conversation usually begins by looking at the instructional goal and learning objectives and brainstorming ideas for game goals that resonate with your target audience. Table 5-1 offers three examples. Each game in the table was for sales representatives, asking players to build something or achieve a specific sales target.

The instructional goal doesn't have anything to do with winning the game. It defines what players will know and be able to do as a result of playing the game. As Table 5-1 illustrates, make sure your game design document lists the target learners, instructional goal, game type, game goal, and core dynamics you plan to use. You can then map your other game design decisions to this goal and core dynamic.

Table 5-1. Examples of How an Instructional Goal Guides Game Design

Formulation Type Matters

Target learners: Sales reps
Instructional goal: Sales reps will use their Fast Facts Guide, along with Deep Dive documents, to provide customers with accurate information on how to resolve or prevent product issues related to formulation type.
Game type: Digital, PC
Game goal: Earn at least $700,000 in sales; maximize your customer ratings while doing it.
Core dynamic: Solve

TE Town

Target learners: Independent distributor reps

Instructional goal: Recognize TE product-selling opportunities across a range of customer and application types, resulting in increased parts sold per customer and new customers. Specific benchmarks:

- Within 12 months, increase the number of parts sold per customer by 12 percent.
- Within two years, increase the number of parts sold per customer by 30 percent.

Game type: Mobile, Casual

Game goal: Construct a town and attain the highest level possible in the game.

Core dynamic: Construct or build (Individual mini games within this larger game had different dynamics, but playing those games helped you build your town and advance to different levels.)

Viropolis

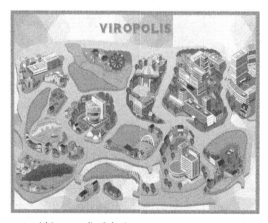

Target learners: Sales reps within a medical device company

Instructional goal: Given specific customer needs and types, execute the sales process appropriately for that customer. This means asking customer-appropriate questions, using customer-appropriate positioning statements, and making customer-appropriate recommendations based on their answers to your questions.

Game type: Tabletop board game

Game goal: Populate a city with the biggest high-rises.

Core dynamics: Solve and construct or build (Players had to solve problems to construct their city.)

As you create game goals for your own learning games, follow these tips:

- Make sure your game goal focuses on the in-game challenge players need to achieve, and your instructional goal focuses on post-play knowledge or behavior change.
- Tailor your game goal to appeal to your target learners and what they need to do in their real-life roles. For example, if they're sales reps, they might have to grow their client base or earn money, make something bigger, or solve something.
- If your game isn't fun, take a look at the game goal. Verify that you have defined an actual challenge that players must overcome or achieve rather than just something players need to complete.

Matching Core Dynamics to Learning Needs

Entertainment games have the luxury of choosing a core dynamic solely because the designers believe it will be fun for players. Learning-game designers should consider whether a particular core dynamic reinforces the real-world context, need, or preferences of target learners. Recall that the core dynamics are the "what" of your game—what players must do to win or how they accomplish the game's challenge.

Table 5-2 reviews definitions of several core dynamics and offers ideas for when you might select one. It also offers tips on which dynamics combine well with others.

Table 5-2. How Core Dynamics Align With Learning Purpose

Core Dynamic	Learning Purpose
Race to the finish: Get to the finish before anyone else or before time runs out. (Candy Land, Mario Kart)	Use this dynamic when your players' real-world application of whatever your game is teaching has a time constraint. It works well in combination with a second dynamic, such as a process that must be completed within a specified period, or a goal that employees must achieve monthly or quarterly.
Territory acquisition: Acquire or take land, typically to create an empire or own the most of something. (Risk, *Civilization*)	Use this dynamic to emulate or make a connection to real-world situations in which dominance is a factor. In-game success increases territory; failure causes it to shrink. This, too, is a great dynamic to pair with another one. This concept correlates well to many real-world situations, such as business success or failure, employee success or failure, or sales success or failure.
Exploration: Wander around and check out various aspects of your game world to see if you can find things of value. (*Tomb Raider*, Clue)	Use this dynamic with learning objectives related to compare and contrast, explain, describe, and analyze. It offers an interesting way for players to acquire information they need to do something else within the game. Consider pairing it with territory acquisition, collection, or race to the finish.

Core Dynamic	Learning Purpose
Collecting: Find and get specified objects. (Trivial Pursuit)	Use this dynamic when you want to help players make associations, such as customer types to specific products, steps in a process to specific tasks that must be performed, and safety behaviors to specific signage.
Rescue or escape: Get out of a situation or place. (Capture the Flag)	Use this dynamic with knowledge recall games in which mastery over knowledge helps players rescue someone or something or escape from someone or something.
Alignment: Arrange game pieces in a particular order. (Candy Crush, Solitaire)	Use this dynamic with learning goals related to helping players identify, recognize, choose, and select. It can be useful when you want to help players put things in order, execute things in sequence, and so on.
Matching: Recognize things that are alike or that fit a specific description; create pairs or groupings. (Spot It, Memory)	Use this dynamic to help players build skill in linking features to benefits, objections to certain customer types, objections and appropriate responses, and so on.
Construct or Build: Create something using specified resources. (Catan, *Minecraft*)	Use this dynamic when you want to reinforce the idea that successful use of knowledge or skill will help players create something in the real world, such as an expanded sales territory and increased business success.
Solution: Solve a problem or puzzle. (Chess, Clue)	Use this dynamic for higher-level thinking or skill practice. It is good for simulation-style problem-solving or role-play activities in which players practice closing a sale, resolving conflicts, making decisions that affect outcomes elsewhere, and so on.

When you are choosing one or two core dynamics for your game, consider whether some core dynamics are better suited to your learning goal than others. Use the ones that make the most sense for your purpose. For example, we developed a game that focused on the challenges of applying company values (excellent communication, ethics, teamwork) while also managing project constraints such as time, money, and regulatory requirements. We used two major dynamics in this game: race to the finish (players had a specific amount of time in which to complete the game) and construct or build (they had to build an object that conformed to specified requirements). These dynamics tightly aligned with their real-world work environment, in which they faced tight time constraints while commercializing a product.

Additionally, think about how your choice will influence players' engagement levels. When you create your initial prototypes for your game, ask yourself, "How would the game change if I changed the dynamic from X to Y?" or "What would happen if I combined two dynamics?" For example, the TE Town game started out with a construct or build dynamic and incorporated a collection dynamic as well (collecting population and treasury). These two worked better together than either would by itself.

Linking Game Mechanics to Learning

Game mechanics are the rules of the game that dictate how players achieve the game goal, interact with other players, and, in digital games, how the system responds to actions they take. Novice game designers tend to make the same mistake when designing their early learning games: They make the rules too complicated. In entertainment games, players will often forgive you if the game play ends up still being fun. This mistake usually torpedoes a learning game, however. People may end up having fun, but their ability to learn becomes compromised. All their brain power goes into figuring out the rules of play, not achieving learning objectives. They also have less tolerance for the frustrations of figuring out how to play. Remember, not all players will be "gamers" who enjoy complexity. Nongamers tend to enjoy games they perceive as easy to learn.

In general, you should link rule complexity with the total time you expect players to be involved in your game. A mini game that takes less than five minutes to play needs to be very easy to learn. A simulation that will last 90 minutes to two hours can have greater complexity. Above all, make sure your game mechanics relate to the learning you want players to be doing and don't detract from it.

Be aware of any game mechanics you choose to enhance the fun that end up hindering learning. It's critical to test and tweak game mechanics. You may think a game mechanic will be great, only to find out in play-testing that it lowers the fun factor or, worse, the learning value. Conversely, you may discover you need to add a game mechanic that you hadn't considered until you watched people play your game.

Adjusting Game Mechanics That Don't Lead to Learning

In early versions of The Knowledge Guru, game play occurred in timed rounds. A round consisted of 10 questions that players had two minutes to answer. Players were penalized for failing to answer all 10 questions within the two minutes. Those who were wildly competitive (and fast readers) liked this mechanic. However, play-testing revealed that most players did not like this mechanic. It actually demotivated them. Even though fast reading wasn't a requirement for the learning objectives within the game, it was a requirement to be successful at the game challenge of becoming a Knowledge Guru. So, we eliminated the time element. Subsequent play-testing showed that the learning experience went way up and the loss of the time element didn't adversely affect players' perceptions of fun. Of course, we also tweaked other mechanics in the process. It took numerous iterations on scoring to get it to a place we, and the players, were happy with.

Table 5-3 offers examples of how game mechanics link to the learning experience.

Table 5-3. How Game Mechanics Link to Learning Experiences

Game	Rule	Link to Learning Need
Formulation Type Matters	Players choose what questions they want to ask the customer. Relevant questions earn players money and increase customer satisfaction ratings. Irrelevant questions decrease customer satisfaction ratings and cost them money.	These rules mimic the real-world experience of sales reps, the target players of the game. Building positive customer feelings requires reps to demonstrate product and customer knowledge. Failing to do so can mean not getting a sale.
Knowledge Guru	If players make a mistake, they see immediate feedback. They must then repeat the question and get it correct before they can progress. Mistakes cost points, with repeated mistakes costing more points than initial ones.	This game mechanic supports two learning principles: repetition helps cement memory, and feedback helps people learn. The system rules help us use two learning principles that work together to make it easier for players to recall information later in their jobs.
A Paycheck Away	Each turn, players must draw a job card. If multiple players are eligible for a job opportunity, they each roll a die. The highest die roll gets the job.	This rule mimics reality: Jobs are hard to get, and multiple people usually compete for a single opening. The rule helps players evaluate whether a job would pay enough if or it was even feasible—for example, perhaps it was not on a bus line and the player doesn't own a car.
A Paycheck Away	At the end of the month, players housed in a homeless shelter must roll a die to see if they can stay in the shelter. If they don't roll a 1 or 6, they lose their shelter housing and must live on the street, check into a pay-by-the-week motel, or pay for permanent housing (which they can only do if they've accrued enough cash in game).	This rule replicates the very harsh reality that homeless shelters typically can only allow residents to stay in emergency shelters for 30 to 60 days. The intent is to help players feel the impact of losing housing, and the associated stress.
A Paycheck Away	Players must draw a "chance" card on every turn. This chance card will result in something good or bad happening, such as their car breaking down, finding $50, or their child getting sick and needing a doctor).	In real life, good and bad events happen daily, most of which have some financial impact. This simulates the difficulty these chance happenings place on a homeless person, whose financial resources are severely constrained.

A Note About Digital Games

Board games and other tabletop games make all the rules explicit. You have a players' guide that people can read before playing or refer to if they get stuck. Digital games usually have players discover the rules as they play or provide tutorials that guide players through their early efforts. They may have a help icon on each screen that players can access if they get stuck. Programmers code these rules into the game so the system creates the most valuable player experience. Here's a few examples from the Knowledge Guru game:

- Do not grant players access to the first level in World A until they complete the tutorial. (Your Guru will direct you as you start the game, providing you with prompts to help you get started.)
- Require players to select a Guru character before they can progress into the game. (Again, you are prompted on what to do here. You can't proceed until you select a character.)
- Allow game administrators to limit players' access to 1) no restrictions, 2) a level per day, 3) a world per day, or 4) a world per week to maximize use of spaced repetition. (Again, unless you played multiple Guru games, you may never realize the game can be set up differently for different use cases.)
- Do not allow players to progress within a level until they correctly respond to a question. (You figure this out as you play. When you first make a mistake, you will discover that you cannot progress until you correctly answer the question.)
- When players make a mistake, present feedback and include a button for them to try again. (This is discovered the first time you make a mistake in the game.)

Using Game Elements

After you choose your game goal, core dynamics, and mechanics, you will begin to select game elements. Some of these will naturally emerge as you start documenting the game's mechanics. Every game has features that keep people engaged; some games have many, others very few. As with your other game design decisions, your choice of what elements to include should be deliberate and made with your instructional goal and objectives in mind.

Let's examine the first 11 in more detail. Chapter 7 will address the 12th one, rewards and scoring. Its complexity warrants an entire chapter.

Conflict

Conflict comes in many forms, but it always represents a challenge for the player to overcome. The challenge could be physical obstacles, combat with another player, or a puzzle that players need to solve. Not every game design needs conflict. For example, Knowledge Guru has limited conflict. There is a challenge—can you get the highest score and become a Guru?—but there is no conflict with the system or other players. In contrast, a game such as Risk has conflict at almost every turn. You go head-to-head with another player as you work to vanquish your opponent.

Questions to ask:

- Given what you want people to learn, what level and amount of conflict is most appropriate? Should you incorporate a conflict that arises with other players, or should you incorporate challenges that all players work together to overcome? Or should you include some sort of challenge against the game itself? For example, puzzle-style games are a challenge that pits the player against the puzzle.
- How can you best represent the real-world conflicts you want people to deal with? For example, in real life, there is often a conflict between time, budget, and quality as people manage a project. How do you represent that conflict within a learning game? (Most often, you will do this through the game mechanics you use.)

Cooperation and Competition

Some games rely on pure competition as an element. Others combine cooperation and competition in some fashion. In cooperative games, the competition is against some other element within the game as opposed to other players. For example, players work together to resolve a challenge in a finite number of turns or timeframe.

In learning games, cooperation is often a better element to use than competition, unless the competition is with the game itself. If you do opt for competition, consider a cooperative element as well, such as having teams of players. You cooperate within your team, but compete against other teams. Direct one-on-one competition with other players can demotivate players or set up a negative dynamic. In contrast, cooperation between players to overcome a game challenge often motivates players and fosters teamwork. In other words, cooperation gets people working together; competition pits people against one another.

In pure competition, only one person or team wins and everyone else loses. The players' focus is very different depending on which element you employ or how you combine the two elements together. Competition can be appropriate, but you need to consider the outcomes it can produce. If you need people to collaborate in the real world, then you should include cooperation as a game element.

For example, we created a game called Access Challenge for a pharmaceutical company. In that game, players compete against other teams—but they work together within their team to try to gain access to a payer system. The competition between teams energized the marketing people and salespeople who played the game, but the cooperation within the team helped develop the internal teamwork required in the real world to negotiate a spot on a formulary.

Questions to ask:

- Do your players need to compete in the real world, or is competition not a factor in using the skill or knowledge you want people to learn?
- If competition is part of the real-world context, do you incorporate it into the

game as players working together to beat the game or as players competing against one another within the game?

- Will competition motivate or demotivate the target group you are designing the game for? What negative consequences might occur if only one person wins and everyone else loses, and how do you manage those emotions?

Strategy and Chance

Strategy puts control into the players' hands; they can make decisions that affect game play or their odds of achieving the goal. Chance takes all the control from the player; they can only react to whatever happens.

Although a game can be heavily weighted toward one or the other, usually games maximize fun by combining strategy and chance. Black Jack is a gambling game that has a huge chance element, but good players can also employ some strategy. Chess is primarily a game of strategy and decision making; the moves you make can limit the amount of chance inherent in your opponent's countermoves. The key for you as a designer is to be intentional in your use of both elements.

Figure 5-2 shows The Global Coaching Challenge, a coaching game we devised for a global company that wanted to reduce its product development and launch timeframe from 10 to 12 years to eight to 10 years. The client thought that better employee coaching was key to reducing this timeline. We also knew, however, that factors outside someone's control could affect the development timeline, so we included chance as an element when designing the game. When players landed on specific spaces on the board, they drew a Coach or Crumble card that positively or negatively influenced their timeline. These cards represented real-world events that happen during product development: an employee needs a transfer back to her home country for family reasons, a product's progress gets halted by regulatory red tape, higher-than-expected revenue increases your budget and enables you to hire another team member. These chance events added to or detracted from your product development cycle time, but you didn't have control over them. You simply had to deal with them once they happened.

Figure 5-2. The Game Board From The Global Coaching Challenge

Image courtesy of Bottom-Line Performance.

Similarly, in A Paycheck Away, we needed to incorporate chance to reflect the real-life issues everyone confronts: children get sick, cars break down, someone decides to help you out. So, players had to draw a chance card on each turn (Figure 5-3).

Figure 5-3. Chance Cards in A Paycheck Away

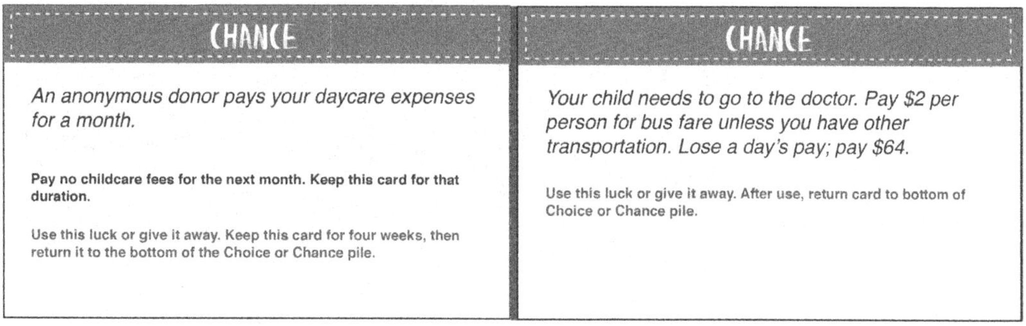

CHANCE	CHANCE
An anonymous donor pays your daycare expenses for a month.	*Your child needs to go to the doctor. Pay $2 per person for bus fare unless you have other transportation. Lose a day's pay; pay $64.*
Pay no childcare fees for the next month. Keep this card for that duration.	Use this luck or give it away. After use, return card to bottom of Choice or Chance pile.
Use this luck or give it away. Keep this card for four weeks, then return it to the bottom of the Choice or Chance pile.	

Image courtesy of Bottom-Line Performance.

Questions to ask:
- Is your game unintentionally creating "win" states that are largely achieved by chance or a specific sequence of events? This can happen more easily than you think. Consider a board game in which the person who got to go first—which was determined by age—had a much greater chance of winning than the person who went last. Players tend to reject games once they realize winning is primarily a result of chance.
- Are you blending strategy and chance in a way that mirrors the skill you want your players to learn, or the context in which they will have to apply the skill?
- What control do players have in the real world over decisions? How do you design that into the game? In the real world, for instance, players may always have access to specific resources. If so, make these resources available in the game you design. Do not leave this aspect of play to chance.
- What chance elements that happen in the real world do you need to mimic in your game?

Aesthetics

Aesthetics, or visuals, are a source of great power in games. Strong visuals can make players curious and positively motivated to play the game, help immerse players in game play, and offer visual cues on what to do. In video games and digital games, aesthetics are a huge part of the game experience and players' perceptions of how fun the game is. If you aren't a graphic designer, you may be tempted to shortchange your game's aesthetics. Don't. Doing so can have a serious negative impact on your players. Weak aesthetics weaken the game experience.

Compare the two game boards in Figure 5-4. Which one would you rather play?

Figure 5-4. Prototype and Professionally Designed Versions of A Paycheck Away

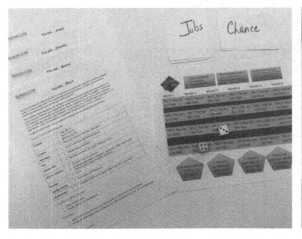

Image courtesy of Bottom-Line Performance.

If you need graphic design help and have room in your budget, consider outsourcing the artwork.

Theme

A theme can add interest and create engagement. It can also be useful in learning games in linking all components of a curriculum, even the nongame elements. For example, we developed a product launch curriculum around a customer's desired racing theme. We created a racing-themed Knowledge Guru game in which players had to complete a series of races to become a Racing Guru (Figure 5-5).

Figure 5-5. Screen From a Racing-Themed Knowledge Guru Game

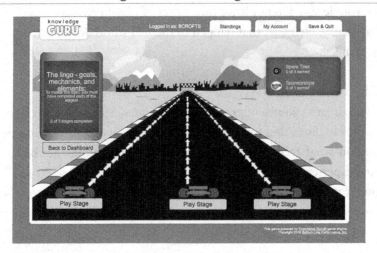

We also created a gamified e-learning course that included a learning activity called Making Fuel, which required learners to blend together the appropriate statements to make fuel for a race car. Then we had learners play a variety of games in the racing-themed launch meeting (Figure 5-6).

Figure 5-6. The Launch Screen for Making Fuel

Story

Stories can be used as a narrative thread woven throughout an entire game. Or stories can be used as a foundation for activities that players do within a learning game. Facts are easier to recall when they are part of a narrative, and stories can inspire and engage. A game can have a theme but no story, a theme and a story, or no story and no theme (think Scrabble). If you elect to create a storyline for your game, keep in mind that a strong story has four elements: characters, plot, tension (or conflict), and resolution.

For example, in A Paycheck Away, story drives game play. Each player draws a character at the start of the game and plays the entire game as that character. Before the game begins, players introduce themselves as their character and share the character's backstory. The plot for that character unfolds through game play, and tension rises as players make decisions and good or bad things happen to them. The resolution occurs at the game's end as we discover if the character makes it into permanent housing.

Questions to ask:
- Should you use a story? Will a story help your game or make it too complicated?
- Should you couple your story with a theme?
- How much story do you need? Do you need just enough to convey a theme, or do you need to immerse players to provide the right learning experience?
- How will you integrate the story into the game experience? Is it something players read beforehand, or do you assign them characters and then let them form the story based on decisions they make?
- Is each player a separate character? Can players choose what character they

want to be, or do they get assigned a character? If so, whom do they represent? Is it a fantasy character (such as a superhero or an alien), or does it represent something with real-world context to their job or situation?

- Are there any nonplaying characters who influence the story? For example, a mining inspector could be portrayed by a deck of cards that players pull from if they roll a certain number on a die (tabletop game) or by clicking a deck to shuffle it (digital game). The mining inspector card might require players to do certain things or affect their progress in the game.

Resources

Resources are tools players get at the start or acquire during game play. In either instance, the resources help players achieve the game goal. Usually resources are limited in some way and become a strategic element as players decide how to gain, use, and manage them. Common resources include money, tools, and building materials. For example, in TE Town, players have two main resources they can acquire: population and treasury. By acquiring population, players increase the sales value of any product they sell. Treasury enables players to purchase amenities for their town, such as parks, museums, and farmer's markets. We deliberately chose population and treasury because they have some correlation to growing customers and earning sales dollars, which sales reps—the target players—care about.

Questions to ask:
- What resources make sense given the skill or knowledge you're trying to teach? Should you have resources that enable people to build or construct something, make decisions, or purchase supplies or other resources?
- Do you need to include currency to represent something, or would that be a distracter? If you are using currency, do you stick with U.S. dollars, or do you use a fictitious form of currency, such as a guilder? (If your game will be a global one, we recommend using U.S. dollars, because we've learned that it translates well globally.)
- Do you need resources in your game?

Time

Time often is a type of resource, but it can take many forms, so it's worth discussing separately. Time can function as a resource you acquire based on how well you perform. It can be something you can purchase, using currency you have. It can also be used as a constraint or a means of compressing real-world time.

Questions to ask:
- How does time factor into your players' jobs? Can you incorporate it into the game in a way that reflects its real-world impact on people? For example, real projects have time limits. By incorporating a time limit into the game, you mimic this constraint.

- Is your real-world learning goal something that people will do over an extended period? If so, can you compress this real-world period into something that makes sense for the game? For example, in A Paycheck Away, the average length of time someone might remain homeless is at least three months. But we do not want a game that requires three months to play; instead, we represent this three-month period in 90 minutes of play. Each 30 minutes represents a month of homelessness in the game.
- How can time hinder learning? Say you want employees to recall information from memory. Putting a timed element on a quiz game to test recall can be detrimental. Remember that we removed the timed element from Knowledge Guru because we wanted an accurate response more than we wanted a speedy one.

Levels

Some games have no explicit levels. (Again, think of Scrabble. Its complexity increases as people play, but no levels are defined.) However, taking time to design your game with levels can have several benefits. It can allow players to play in a tutorial mode first and then advance to more difficult play as they build skill. It can enable people of varying abilities to all play and compete in the same game. Levels can also be a motivating influence to players if they equate higher levels with greater in-game status. We've seen acquiring the status of Knowledge Guru (gained by progressing through many levels of play) as a symbol in some employee groups. People want to be on the Guru leaderboard and earn the title.

Work on Your Own

Before you start designing your own learning game, take time to thoroughly break down a learning game. You did this at a high level in chapter 3, when we first introduced you to learning games. Now that you've finished this chapter, you have a much better idea of the decisions a good learning-game designer makes about game design. Do one of these activities:

- Re-evaluate one of the learning games you've already played and see if you can identify how game design decisions about game goals, core dynamics, game mechanics, and game elements link to learning objectives.
- Choose a brand-new learning game and do the same thing.

Wrap-Up

As a learning-game designer, you will make many choices about your game's design. Make sure they are purposeful ones that balance fun with your instructional goal and learning objectives. Your primary focus is helping people learn, so make sure your design decisions all support learning—or at least don't hinder it.

Consult the learning game design template in appendix 5. Add to the game design you started in chapter 4. Use the question prompts next to the game design elements to help you think through your game's design and connect it to learning needs.

Two Game Design Case Studies

In This Chapter
✓ Case study: Mosaic's Feed the World board game
✓ Case study: TE Connectivity's TE Town mobile game
✓ Guru game play opportunity

Chapter 5 walked you through all you need to consider when designing your game: the game goal, the core dynamic, mechanics, and game elements. This chapter summarizes two learning games so you can see examples of game design choices and the learning rationale behind them.

Case Study: Feed the World

Feed the World is a board game we created for the phosphate-mining company Mosaic. The game helped Bottom-Line Performance and Mosaic win Gold for Best Advance in Compliance Training in the 2016 Brandon Hall Excellence in Learning Awards (Boller 2016).

Feed the World serves as the final activity of a five-day new employee orientation program (Figure 6-1). Every employee—not just those who will work on mining sites—must complete 24 hours of safety training before starting their job duties. Because new hires are not allowed onto Mosaic's worksite before receiving this training, all onboarding activities need to occur in the classroom.

The game's target players include anyone hired to work at Mosaic. When crafting a persona for the game, we found that typical players would be male, between the ages of 40 and 55, and high school graduates. They also would have likely worked in a similar industry before being hired at Mosaic.

Figure 6-1. Game Board for Feed the World

Game Description

The game takes about two hours to play and gives players an opportunity to recall and practice using content covered in the previous days' training. The game goal is for players to work together to feed an ever-increasing world population, achieving production goals each year. The learning goal is for players to recall all the safety steps and environmental protection steps covered throughout the workshop and identify the appropriate resources required to execute those steps.

To play an entire game, players complete four rounds, which represents four years of actual mining production. Each round has seven turns and represents one calendar year of mining effort. The seven turns within a round of play align with the seven steps required to get phosphate from the mine to food producers. The first two rounds feature a lower production goal than the final two rounds, so the game difficulty increases as the game progresses. The number of people players must feed in the game matches the real-world increases required to feed the world's population.

Appendix 6 has the rules for Feed the World setup and game play.

Game Design Decisions and Learning

The design team made numerous decisions about the game's design based on the learning goals they wanted players to achieve and the context in which they would need to recall this information in their jobs. Table 6-1 identifies game design decisions and their link to learning needs and goals.

Table 6-1. Feed the World

Game Design Decision	Link to Learning and Job Context
Game title: Feed the World.	This correlates with the company's mission.
Progression within a round of play (seven turns to finish one round).	Throughout the workshop, a learning map (which converts into a game board on the final day) focuses on the seven steps of the mining process.
Rounds that correlate to a calendar year and the requirement that the amount of phosphate players must mine increases each round.	World population is increasing each year, so more people must be fed. The game requirement reinforces this situation.
Scenario cards drive players forward through the seven turns in a round. A player draws a card and reads the scenario aloud. Before deciding what to do, the player can discuss the scenario with all other players. After hearing ideas from the group, the player makes a decision. Players can then flip the card to compare their response to the correct response (Figure 6-2).	Collaboration, not competition, is required in players' actual jobs. A collaborative game mirrors the real-world behavior Mosaic wants in the workplace.
Each scenario card requires players to identify what resources they need to resolve the scenario (Figure 6-2).	The workshop covered several resources employees will use on the worksite to maintain safety. The game reinforces them and requires learners to apply what they learned.
For the scoring mechanism, players collect phosphate crystals when they are successful. They then use the crystals to fill in the scoring grid, which shows progress in feeding the target population.	Scoring correlates to what Mosaic produces and to its mission of feeding the world.
The game aesthetics illustrate the seven steps of the mining process.	This illustration reinforces everything taught in the workshop.
An element of chance appears in this game: Players can draw mining inspection cards that can have a positive or negative impact on scoring (Figure 6-2).	The cards represent typical "chance" elements on the job, such as the an unannounced mining inspection from an OSHA employee.

Figure 6-2. Game Design Decisions

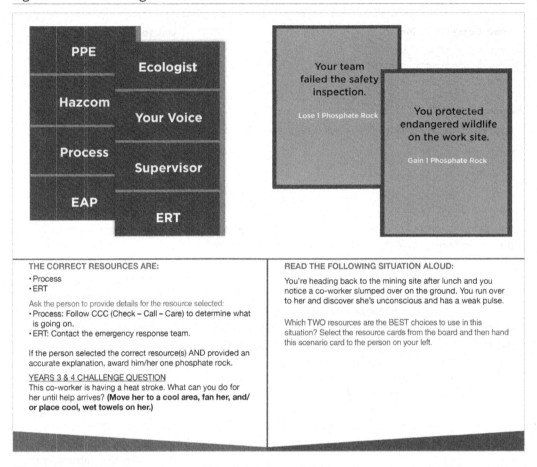

THE CORRECT RESOURCES ARE:
- Process
- ERT

Ask the person to provide details for the resource selected:
- Process: Follow CCC (Check – Call – Care) to determine what is going on.
- ERT: Contact the emergency response team.

If the person selected the correct resource(s) AND provided an accurate explanation, award him/her one phosphate rock.

YEARS 3 & 4 CHALLENGE QUESTION
This co-worker is having a heat stroke. What can you do for her until help arrives? **(Move her to a cool area, fan her, and/or place cool, wet towels on her.)**

READ THE FOLLOWING SITUATION ALOUD:

You're heading back to the mining site after lunch and you notice a co-worker slumped over on the ground. You run over to her and discover she's unconscious and has a weak pulse.

Which TWO resources are the BEST choices to use in this situation? Select the resource cards from the board and then hand this scenario card to the person on your left.

Top left: Resources that players must consider using to successfully respond to each scenario. PPE stands for personal protective equipment. EAP stands for emergency action plan, and ERT stands for emergency response team. *Top right:* Mining Inspector cards provide an element of chance in the game. *Bottom:* An example of the front and back of a scenario card. Players work together to decide on the best response to the scenario. After making a decision, the card reader flips the card over to see the correct response.

Case Study: TE Town

TE Town is a smartphone game designed for independent distributor representatives who sell TE Connectivity products along with the products of several other manufacturers. TE Connectivity wanted TE Town to help:

- Make TE's products top of mind for the sales reps.
- Get reps to think in terms of "customer types" rather than in terms of specific customer names or industries. A customer type references the kind of product applications a customer may find relevant. For example, a medical device manufacturer may fit into the customer type called "handheld devices." This type might also include a company that manufactures cell phones, one that manufactures handheld printers, and one that manufactures digital cameras.

TE's products have such breadth that they can be used in a huge array of product applications. Therefore, TE needed to build recognition of customer types and the product applications associated with each customer type.

- Expand the number of products sold to individual customers. As reps' understanding of the array of product technologies housed within a single device grew, they could expand the number of products they sold to a single customer.

Game Description

Players are elected mayor of TE Town when they log in to the game (Figure 6-3, left). Their game goal is to upgrade their towns to the highest level possible. Each upgrade they make to their town moves them up a level in the game. The learning goals are for distributor reps to accurately identify three to five customer types and specify the product technologies associated with each of them. Once a product technology is identified, distributor reps should be able to identify appropriate product families relevant for that customer type.

Figure 6-3. TE Town

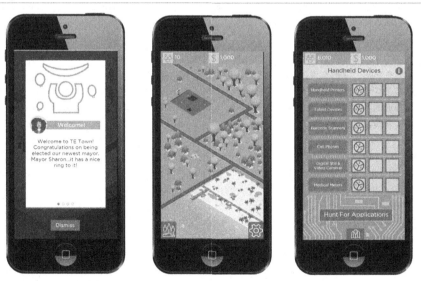

Left: The welcome screen for TE Town. *Middle:* Undeveloped plots. *Right:* Customer type grid for handheld devices.

When players enter the game, they can scroll around to see a wide swath of undeveloped plots (Figure 6-3, middle). They begin developing their town by selecting a region. To access it, they must assign it a customer type. This unlocks a customer type grid that they populate by playing a mini game called Hunt for Applications (Figure 6-3, right). Through playing and replaying this game, players gradually build their knowledge of the product applications associated with the customer type. Once they populate their grid with product applications, they gain access to other mini games that help them build knowledge of product technologies associated with each product application within the customer type.

As players acquire and demonstrate mastery of customer types, product applications, and product families, they can build the population and earn treasury dollars that enable them to upgrade their towns. This, in turn, advances them through the levels in the game.

Game Design Decisions and Learning

Despite the complex game design, every game design decision was in support of learners' needs and desired learning outcomes. Table 6-2 reviews some of the key game design decisions we made and how these decisions support learning.

Table 6-2. TE Town

Game Design Decision	Link to Learning and Job Context
After consulting with the client and learning about its highly mobile distributor representatives, we opted to create a game designed for mobile first. We wanted a game that let players make meaningful progress with only a few minutes of play required per session.	Field-based sales representatives use their smartphones more than other devices. Time is also precious, mostly available to them in small chunks. So, if game play sessions are short, reps are more apt to play. They'll also be able to play it when it's most relevant, such as in the minutes before meeting a client.
Players become mayor of a fictitious town. Success in the game helps them build population, which in turn increases their treasury. Treasury then gets used to upgrade the town as they build.	Reps think about territories and how to build them, and about acquiring commission revenue and growing customers. This dynamic complemented this framework, but didn't mirror it, lending the game an element of fantasy. Research shows fantasy has a powerful, positive effect on learning, helping learners feel safe while playing and take risks within the game (Lepper 1988; Malone 1981).
Requiring only a few minutes to play, every mini game helps the player build population or earn treasury dollars. Players repeat a sequence of three mini games for each product application they have within their grid. All mini games linked to a specific product application enable players to build treasury.	The mini games for each product application build on one another, reinforcing content through repetition. These mini games work together to help sales reps learn: • specific customer types • product applications relevant to a specific customer type • product families relevant to a specific product application • useful questions to ask customers to identify needs • tools that can help them sell products.

Game Design Decision	Link to Learning and Job Context
We wanted to build in an element of surprise and variety, so we included a "limited availability" mini game called Sales Scramble. Sales Scramble is a timed game that is mostly for fun. Players can access this game only twice within each customer type. It's more challenging to play, and players do not get repeat tries at it.	Sales Scramble provides more fun than learning—or, as we call it, "learning light." However, it does help players build population. The more population a player has, the more value each sale has in terms of growing treasury. This treasury, in turn, enables players to upgrade their towns. It adds an element of challenge that keeps players engaged in the other parts of the game that are more "learning heavy."

Guru Game Play Opportunity

To reinforce the concepts in this chapter, play the Learning Design and Game Design level in Game Design Guru (www.theknowledgeguru.com/ATDGameDesignGuru).

Wrap-Up

The two case studies illustrate that game design for learning is purposeful design. Both examples demonstrate how the game design team made its decisions for game goals, core dynamics, rules, and game elements based on what they wanted the learning outcomes of the game to be. Every decision then needed to be tested to ensure that players would find the game fun to play while also gaining the knowledge and skills they needed.

Chapter 7 completes the section on game design fundamentals by introducing you to the nuances of designing scoring and rewards for learning games.

Matching Scoring to Learning Goals

In This Chapter
✓ What are the basics of scoring for learning game design?
✓ What scoring methods can you use in your game?
✓ How do you create a scoring system?
✓ Three scoring case studies
✓ Guru game play opportunity

When players sit down to a game, most instinctively know that the goal of playing is to win, whether it is accomplished by collecting the most resources, crossing the finish line first, or finding the treasure before everyone else. Game designers don't have to tell players the goal of the game is to win. However, good game designers do explain to players how they earn the points and achievements that allow them to win. For example, players need to know the conditions for crossing the finish line or finding the treasure. Success or failure at in-game activities feeds into both winning the game and determining the score. This chapter explores how to create scoring within your game (Figure 7-1).

Figure 7-1. Learning-Game Design Process: Scoring and Rewards

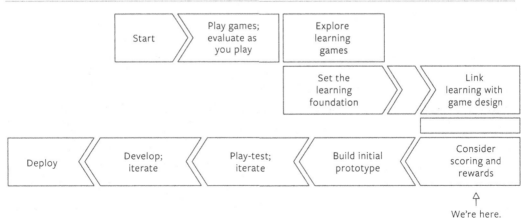

Points and achievements inform players where they are in the game, how close they might be to winning, how close other players are to winning, and how they should form a strategy. But scoring provides more than a record of who wins; it also provides a guideline for performance and activities within the game. In fact, scoring in a learning game needs to correlate to how well or poorly a player is performing in the game. The scoring algorithm you create as the game designer needs to tie to both learning and player progress in the game. It also should reflect on-the-job behaviors and thought processes you want to teach and reinforce.

Scoring Basics

Scoring in a learning game should revolve around six key concepts.

Keep the Scoring Simple

You do not want to create complex scoring algorithms that require players to consult the guidebook repeatedly. Instead, the focus needs to be on learning. It can be as simple as a card game in which players "score" by collecting cards, with the winner being the person with the most cards at the end of the game (Figure 7-2).

Figure 7-2. Challenge and Answer Cards for a Learning Game

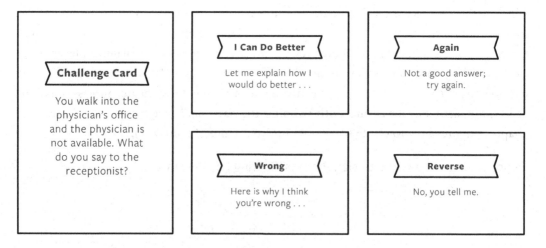

Make the Scoring Transparent

Anyone playing the game should be able to figure out how to score and what it takes to win the game. If some mystery or uncertainty surrounds how a score is obtained, the learners may get confused or frustrated because they won't know how their actions in the game are reflected in the score. Make it clear in the opening tutorial, rulebook, or explanation screen how scoring is achieved.

Tie the Scoring Directly to Learning Outcomes

If players are learning the content in the game, they should be doing well in terms of score; if they are not learning, their score should reflect this. You can't let chance dictate winning in a learning game. The goal is mastery or reinforcement of the content through game play, which can be difficult elements to balance. However, you must ensure that learning is the ultimate outcome, and nothing drives a player's actions more in a game than scoring.

De-Emphasize Winning in Learning Environments

If you are using competition as a game element, make it clear that winning or losing is low in importance compared with learning (Cantador and Conde 2010). You don't want to make the losing experience so terrible that it turns off the loser, and you don't want the game so focused on winning that everything else is forgotten. Learning games need to be about learning—not winning. So be careful when crafting the winning state of an instructional game so that even if players or their teams do not win, they still learn.

Add Variability to the Scoring

This usually means that scoring cannot be one-dimensional. For example, if you create a question-and-answer game and players get the same points for answering questions correctly, then they all could have identical scores at the end if no one misses a question. This scoring algorithm would make it difficult to create a leaderboard or competition because everyone can achieve the same score. So a good game designer might add another variable, such as time or number of tries required: The score could be a combination of how many questions a player answered correctly on the first try and how long it took to answer all the questions. This combination allows two players to learn the content but not necessarily obtain the same score.

Reinforce On-the-Job Realities Through the Scoring

Actions and activities required for an effective performance should be echoed or mimicked within the scoring. You do not want the scoring of the game to work against what the player is attempting to learn. For example, if the player's job requires accuracy, the game should require accuracy to win. If the player's job does not include time pressures, making time part of the scoring algorithm is not an effective game mechanic. The scoring should not hinder learning or transfer to the job. Design the scoring mechanism of the game to reward the behaviors and activities required for effective on-the-job performance.

Methods of Scoring

Scoring is about more than points; it provides feedback on how well a person is doing in the game. In a learning game, scoring should help players gauge their progress toward mastery of the content. As such, achievements and rewards can come in several different forms.

Earning Points

Points are feedback related to the level of effort, timeliness, correctness, or accuracy of responses to a question, scenario, or other instructional event. They are effective for providing a means of measuring progress against a standard, the maximum amount of points attainable, or peers. Typically, you want a high level of points. So instead of assigning one point for a correct answer, assign 100 points. The larger the point value, the more players will feel is at stake. Getting one point for answering a question does not seem as big of a deal as getting 100 points, even though the overall results might be the same. This is also true of losing one point versus 100 points. Additionally, adding a large number of points allows you to create more variability within the scoring.

Leveling Up

In many learning games, a level is a defined phase that requires certain actions to move to the next phase. Sometimes a level equates to mastery of content in one area, sometimes it represents a player completing a certain set of tasks, and sometimes each level in a game is tied to one overarching instructional objective. Leveling up, or progressing from the simplest level to more complex ones, creates a learning environment that mirrors moving from simple knowledge to more complex knowledge.

Levels also keep the learning space manageable. Developing a learning game with one vast level containing all the content and dozens of learning objectives would be daunting for both the player and the designer. A well-designed progression of levels accomplishes three goals:

1. Levels help players progress by providing new information or insights at each level. This in turn keeps players engaged and focused on a relatively small learning objective.
2. Levels build on and reinforce skills or knowledge developed in the previous level. As players progress and the levels become more difficult, they are required to recall and use knowledge or skills learned in previous levels to advance. However, at this point, they usually have to perform the skills more quickly or under greater pressure to make the application of the skill more challenging. Toward the end, players usually must use skills learned from previous levels in unique combinations.
3. Levels serve as motivation. Progression through the levels becomes a goal players want to attain. The different levels provide small, achievable goals that encourage players to do more activities so they can get to the next level. Progression through all levels means players have achieved terminal learning objectives.

Unlocking Content

Games can reward success by giving learners access to places within the game space that they earn through productive game play. This reward mechanism taps into people's desire to explore. Another version of this reward structure is when in-game mysteries are revealed based on players' performance, or they earn clues to solve in-game puzzles. If learners do well, they might earn the right to play more of the game. This might mean earning an extra life, an extra chance, or even a reward like a power-up, which gives players special powers for a short time.

Power-Ups

Game Design Guru uses power-ups that you can earn as you play a level within the game. The game includes several different power-ups that players earn based on performance. Watch for them as you play the game.

Earning Achievements

Whether they are badges, trophies, or other visible signs of accomplishment, achievements in learning games can encourage players to perform a specific behavior or task, or to progress through different levels. Achievements that happen in a competitive game can also help keep players from feeling totally shut out if they lose. They can show players that they did indeed learn while playing the game.

Figure 7-3 is an example of an achievement case from a game. Notice there is space for numerous achievements, all of which players earn based on how well they perform within the game.

Figure 7-3. Scoring in a Game With Numerous Achievements

Learning games have two categories of achievements: measurement achievements and completion achievements. Learners receive measurement achievements for completing a task to a certain degree against other learners' performance, their own performance, or another standard. For example, many games use a three-star rating system, which gives players one to three stars based on how well they performed on a level. One star indicates adequate performance on a level; three stars means the top level of performance.

Stars and Performance Ratings

Game Design Guru uses a three-star system to rate your performance. If you respond to all questions within a level without mistakes, you earn three stars. If you make numerous mistakes as you play, you only earn one star. Note that the game allows you to replay to earn all three stars.

Completion achievements do not tell players how well they have performed the task; instead, the game offers these achievements once learners complete a task. Completion achievements can be split into two subcategories: performance-contingent achievements, which require skill or knowledge to complete, and non-performance-contingent achievements, which are awarded for simply being present. The best practice from a learning-game perspective is to use measurement achievements instead of completion achievements to increase a player's motivation to play the game. However, if you have to use completion achievements, use performance-contingent achievements.

Creating the Scoring Algorithm

Creating a scoring system is more difficult than it might appear. This is especially true if you are creating an online game. Because online games can calculate scores and keep track of variables, their scoring can get complicated quickly. To manage this complexity, use a spreadsheet when developing the scoring process. With a spreadsheet, you can see how manipulating points for one item affects an overall ideal score. Or you can see if a player is even capable of achieving enough points to level up or earn a critical badge.

Table 7-1 is an example spreadsheet showing scoring for different types of questions within an adventure game, with points awarded based on the degree of difficulty. These three questions represent the challenge in level 1. If players answer all questions for three question types correctly, they could earn 14,500 points; they need 10,000 to advance to level 2.

Creating a chart like this can help you create a fair system for awarding points for specific activities. Often a spreadsheet is the best way to arrange this type of information because you can then change the numbers for scoring and observe the corresponding results.

Table 7-1. Scoring and Levels of Difficulty

Level	Activity	Degree of Difficulty	Points	Number Available to Answer on Level	Total Possible Points per Question Type
1	Answer Challenge Question	Hard	1,000	3	3,000
1	Average Question	Intermediate	800	10	8,000
1	Opening Question	Easy	700	5	3,500
				Total Possible Level Points	14,500
				Points Needed to Move to Next Level	10,000

For example, one mistake that new learning-game designers make is that they devise the in-game challenges and scoring in such a way that unless players are perfect, they are unable to move to the next level. On the other hand, game designers sometimes allow players to earn too many points in the beginning, and the game becomes too easy. Creating a proper scoring structure is important to balance an instructional game.

Also, notice in Table 7-1 that players do not lose points for incorrect answers. If you add in penalties for incorrect answers, the spreadsheet and the scoring become more difficult. You would need to determine how many points can be lost for each incorrect answer to still achieve your learning goals.

For example, if players lost 1,000 points for each incorrect hard question above, they could still make it to the next level if they answered every other intermediate and easy question correctly. In this case, that may be acceptable. However, if the hard questions were a synthesis of knowledge to be learned, it may be important from a learning perspective that the hard questions be answered correctly. In that case, losing 1,000 points for each wrong answer would not be enough. The designer might want to make the penalty higher so the player cannot advance without answering at least one or two of the hard questions correctly.

Start with a simple spreadsheet with scores for correct answers or actions and then add complexity as you build the game. Keep in mind that you want to strive for simple scoring, but you must make scoring meaningful and motivating as well. The action or knowledge that leads to scoring will be the actions the players will focus on when playing the game.

As you consider crafting your scoring algorithm for your game, here are some best practices to keep in mind:

- Reward players for boring tasks and give them feedback for interesting ones.
- Make achievements challenging for the greatest returns in player performance.
- If you choose to give rewards, give them for performance rather than completion. Giving players a badge for completing a section isn't a good idea.

It's better to give a reward if they complete the section to a certain standard of proficiency.

- Let your reward be a form of performance feedback to the player.
- For complex tasks requiring creativity or complicated strategies, or when onboarding a new player into the game, instill a mastery orientation. In other words, have players be concerned with improving their own skills and abilities during the game experience rather than comparing their abilities with others.
- For simple or repetitive tasks, instill a performance orientation. In other words, have players compare their scores or knowledge gained with others.
- Use expected achievements—achievements players know they are going to receive if they perform in a certain manner—as a method for players to set goals. Use unexpected achievements to encourage exploration within the game environment.
- If competitive achievements are used in the game, make them available only after the players have learned how to play and are comfortable with the game and scoring function.
- Consider adding cooperative achievements to encourage players to work together.
- Align the activities and actions on the job with the actions in the game for best learning and transferability.
- Play-test your game to find out if your scoring is increasing player motivation, decreasing it, or having no influence at all.

Designing Scoring Is Harder Than Meets the Eye

Even with a simple game, such as Password Blaster, the scoring may not be as simple from a design perspective as you would think. If you have played the game, you may have noticed that the higher on the screen you shot the weak password, the more points you earned. The game's designers had to create an algorithm to determine a descending score structure from the top of the screen to the bottom. This algorithm involved counting the number of pixels down from the top of the screen that an individual password had fallen and then deciding on the right score. Not as easy as it seems.

While you may not program a game like this yourself and outsource development instead, you still have to have a vision and plan for the scoring that the programmer can implement.

With some tips on scoring methods and algorithms in mind, let's examine how game designers created the scoring framework for three learning games you're now familiar with: Zombie Sales Apocalypse, Knowledge Guru, and TE Town.

Zombie Sales Apocalypse

The Zombie Sales Apocalypse game features many scoring elements simultaneously. First, the game bases players' overall score on the number of questions they answer correctly minus the number of questions they answer incorrectly. The questions are embedded in dialogue, and a wrong choice in the dialogue reduces the players' score.

Next, the game scores players across five dimensions of the sales model. In this case, points are not rewarded; instead, meters are filled for each selection of dialogue that correctly fulfills the element of the meter. When a meter is filled, players have successfully completed all the dialogue related to that element of the sales model. Table 7-2 shows what it looks like in a spreadsheet, and Figure 7-4 shows what it looks like on the screen.

Table 7-2 indicates how the scoring structure was designed. First, each element of the sales model was identified and listed and then linked to specific dialogue used within the game. The player selects the correct dialogue for the character to say from a list of three possible answers. Each right or wrong answer is assigned a score. Right answers increase the score; wrong answers decrease it. The total possible points and total possible penalty points are calculated to make sure the game is balanced in scoring. (This table changed many times while trying to create the right balance for scoring.)

Table 7-2. Zombie Sales Apocalypse Scoring Table

Elements of Sales Model	Dialogue 1: Correct Answer Points	Dialogue 2: Correct Answer Points	Dialogue 3: Correct Answer Points	Dialogue 4: Correct Answer Points	Total Possible Points	Wrong Answer Penalty	Possible Wrong Answers	Total Possible Penalty Points
Problem Identification	1,000				1,000	500	4	2,000
Client Knowledge	1,000		1,000		2,000	500	4	2,000
Persistence		1,000	1,000		2,000	500	5	2,500
Product Knowledge			1,000	1,000	2,000	500	6	3,000
Professionalism				1,000	2,000	500	5	2,500
Totals	**2,000**	**1,000**	**3,000**	**2,000**	**9,000**	**2,500**		**12,000**

In Figure 7-4, you can see how the scoring looks in the game. On the left side of the screen, you can see meters and the initial score. The score increases or decreases based on how the player answers a particular question. At the end of the game, the score is provided to the player.

Figure 7-4. How Scoring From a Table Translates Into a Game

Knowledge Guru

Knowledge Guru has a relatively simple scoring system, but it still requires more complexity than you might imagine. Two needs drive this complexity: to ensure good variability in player scores for the leaderboards, and to align with the learning goals of the game and reward players for performance over time. Table 7-3 shows how each question is scored in Knowledge Guru. At this point, the scoring is simple. Table 7-4 details where greater complexity emerges. To ensure scoring variability, we created power-ups and other rewards.

The Guru game platform is based on the cognitive science concept that repetition builds long-term memory. Each learning objective within the game has at least one question set, which is a series of three questions that ask the player to recall or apply the same content to correctly respond to a question. On players' initial exposure to the question content, which is the first question in the set, the value of a correct response is 1,000 points. The penalty for making a mistake is a 250-point deduction to their score. The game requires players to retry until they correctly respond. If players correctly respond on their first retry, they earn the full value of the question.

However, by players' third exposure to the question content, the value of the question is much higher (10,000 points), and thus a mistake results in players losing 10,000 points. A correct response on a subsequent attempt only nets players 5,000 points. Tables 7-3 and 7-4 show what the full scoring algorithm looks like, including the bonus points for each "bonus gate" game and the possible values when players earn power-ups.

Table 7-3. Scoring for the Knowledge Guru Game

World A Actions	Points Gained and Lost
Respond correctly on first attempt at question	1,000
Respond incorrectly on first attempt at question	–250
Retry responding after reviewing misstep	1,000
Miss second attempt at question	–500
Respond correctly on third attempt at question	1,000
Miss any future attempts	–500
Answer correctly on fourth attempt or more	0
World B Actions	**Points Gained and Lost**
Respond correctly on first attempt at question	5,000
Respond incorrectly on first attempt at question	–2,500
Retry responding after reviewing misstep	2,500
Miss second attempt at question	–5,000
Respond correctly on third attempt at question	0
Miss any future attempts	–5,000
Answer correctly on fourth attempt or more	0
World C Actions	**Points Gained and Lost**
Respond correctly on first attempt at question	10,000
Respond incorrectly on first attempt at question	–10,000
Retry responding after reviewing misstep	5,000
Miss second attempt at question	–20,000
Respond correctly on third attempt at question	0
Miss any future attempts	–20,000
Answer correctly on fourth attempt or more	0

Table 7-4. Power-Up and Reward Scoring for Knowledge Guru Game

Power-Up or Reward	How to Earn	Frequency	Effect	How to Lose	Value
Maximizer (Worlds B and C Only)	Earned within first percentage of questions on a specquest in each world. If you have 3 questions, given at 1. If you have 10 questions, given at 2-3.	Dependent on number of topics: 6-7 topics = 3; 4-5 = 2; 3 = 1. ~50%, rounded down of topic count with a minimum of 1.	Once earned, keeping it through the entire quest will triple the value of the final question.	Miss any question after earning it.	15,000 (World B), 30,000 (World C).

Table 7-4. Power-Up and Reward Scoring for Knowledge Guru Game ·

Power-Up or Reward Name	How to Earn	Frequency	Effect	How to Lose	Value
Safety (All Worlds)	Given as incentive to replay a quest.	This is not an "earned" power-up. It is automatically available on any level in which player didn't get a 3-star performance.	Guards against one miss. Missing a question will result in no score change and no other power-ups will be lost.	Miss any question after earning it.	None. It simply keeps you from losing points.
Simplifier (World A Only)	Same as a maximizer or doubler.	Same as a maximizer or doubler.	Removes one distracter on next question.	Used immediately.	None. It merely makes a question easier; this is only available in World A.
Doubler (All Worlds)	Randomly gifted on getting a question correct (maximum of 3 per world; 1 max in a quest; shows up before last question).	Same as a maximizer or simplifier.	Doubles value of next question.	Answer the next question.	2,000 (World A), 10,000 (World B), 20,000 (World C).
Perfect Level (All Worlds)	Earned after achieving a perfect score (no misses) within a level.	1 per level.	Add value to score depending on world.	This is a reward.	1,000 (World A), 5,000 (World B), 10,000 (World C).
Perfect World (All Worlds)	Finish all levels and bonus gate perfectly in a world.	1 per world.	Add double max value of questions in entire world.	Any miss.	(Your total world value + selected bonus gate value) * 2.
Bonus Gate Game	Finish all levels within a world.	1 per world.	Depends on player choice.	Make a mistake.	Depends on "bet" made, and ranges from 1,500 to 13,500.

TE Town Scoring

TE Town went through five iterations of the scoring. Items we started with—but had deleted by the time we got to this version—included penalties for absence from the game and a variety of bonuses players could collect based on how well they performed in various mini games. The scoring was simply getting too complex to easily communicate to players. When we play-tested, we found players were not clear on how they were earning population or treasury dollars, so we kept refining the scoring and our in-game communication until we reached a point in which the majority of players easily understood what was happening. Table 7-5 shows the final scoring.

Table 7-5. Scoring Algorithm for TE Town Mobile Game

	Starting Population	Treasury
	10	$1,000.00
Mini Game 1: Hunt for Applications		
Player Action	**Population Gained or Lost**	**Treasury Gained or Lost**
Shoot a correct application.	Max of 1,000; value decreases the longer player waits to shoot the application.	N/A
Shoot an incorrect application or miss one that is correct.	Lose a life; lose three lives and game over.	N/A
Mini Game 2: Meet the Customer		
Player Action	**Population Gained or Lost**	**Treasury Gained or Lost**
Bid 1: Get it right.	0	250
Bid 2: Get both right.	0	500
Bid 3: Get all right.	0	1,000
Miss any question.	0	0
Mini Game 3: Product Picker		
Player Action	**Impact on Item's Sales Value**	**Multiplier**
Right on first try.	100% of sale value.	0.25 (25 cents) per townie
Second attempt.	Lose 60% of sale value.	0.1 (10 cents) per townie
Third attempt.	Lose 80% of sale value.	0.5 (5 cents) per townie
All subsequent attempts.	Lose 96% of sale value.	0.01 (1 cent) per townie

Table 7-5. Scoring Algorithm for TE Town Mobile Game

Mini Game 4: Seal the Deal		
Player Action	**Population Gained or Lost**	**Treasury Gained or Lost**
Ask a good question without asking any bad questions.	0	0.25 (25 cents) per townie
Ask a good question after asking one bad question.	0	0.05 (5 cents) per townie
Ask a good question after asking two bad questions.	0	0.01 (1 cent) per townie
Mini Game 5: Sales Scramble		
Game Action	**Population Gained or Lost**	**Treasury Gained or Lost**
People moving into town when game begins.	2,000	0
After 9 seconds elapse.	1,600	0
After 18 seconds elapse.	1,200	0
After 27 seconds elapse.	800	0
After 36 seconds elapse.	400	0
After 45 seconds elapse without success.	0	0

Guru Game Play Opportunity

We invite you to return to the Game Design Guru game and play the level covering scoring and rewards. Remember, go to www.theknowledgeguru.com/ATDGameDesignGuru and play to learn!

Wrap-Up

Scoring is one of the most difficult elements to get right when creating a learning game. As a designer, you must balance the need to reward appropriate skills or behaviors while trying to provide a disincentive for incorrect responses. You need to craft the scoring system so that it's fair to the player but also easy to understand and master. By using a spreadsheet and mapping out scores that would result in various scenarios, you can work toward a fair and balanced scoring algorithm for your learning game.

But don't make the scoring aspect of your game more complicated than it needs to be; otherwise, it will interfere with learning. In fact, the simpler, the better. Most important, scores in learning games must be an indication of learning.

Part 3

Putting Game Design Knowledge to Work

Creating the First Prototype

In This Chapter

✓ What is a prototype?
✓ How do you craft a prototype?
✓ How does prototyping differ for digital games?
✓ Work on your own

Now it's time to put together all the knowledge you've gained from previous chapters and create the first version, or prototype, of your game. Figure 8-1 shows you where we are.

Figure 8-1. Learning-Game Design Process: Build Initial Prototype

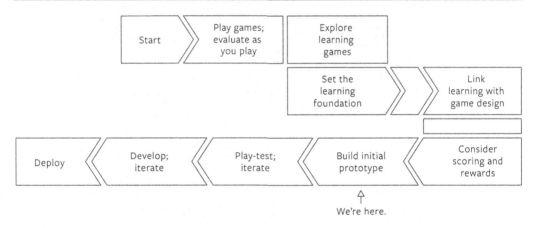

We're here.

What Is a Prototype?

In game design, a prototype is the first playable version of your game, not the complete version. Simplified and rudimentary, it contains enough actual content for you to evaluate the game's learning value for your target audience and whether your game idea is fun for others. Your goal with a prototype is to create a quick, easy, and low-cost test of your game design idea.

A game prototype helps you answer the following questions:

- Is your game idea engaging? Do people like the core dynamic?
- Are your game mechanics and game elements engaging? Do you have too many? Not enough? What should you add, change, or remove?
- Is the learning experience effective? Will game play enable people to achieve the learning objectives you have defined for the game?

The cheapest, easiest, and fastest prototyping tool for you to use is paper, even if your ultimate goal is to create a digital game. While the idea of a paper prototype for board or card games makes sense, some people resist using paper to prototype a digital or video solution. It's tempting to mock it up in a digital tool, particularly if you are the coder or artist, or just like messing around in PowerPoint or other digital slide-creation tools.

You should resist the temptation, however. Prototyping on paper prevents lots of rework later, and it helps you quickly spot problems you might miss with digital prototypes. Paper prototyping forces you to carefully think through the player interactions and game mechanics. Figures 8-2 and 8-3 show examples of paper prototypes for a board game and a mobile game, respectively. Note that the mobile game prototype has been designed with moveable parts so that a user can actually test it and simulate the system interactions.

Figure 8-2. Prototype for a Board Game

Figure 8-3. Prototype for a Mobile Game

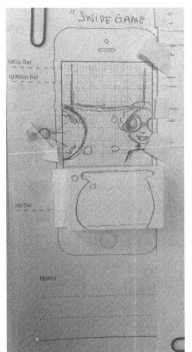
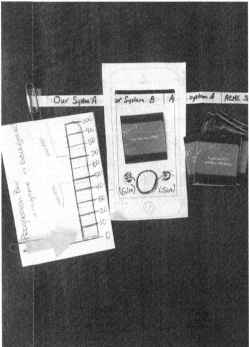

Crafting a Prototype

Prototyping works best when done as a team with two to four people. The prototyping team should not include the client, whether internal or external, at this stage. Instead, consider involving a game designer, the project manager, a writer, and perhaps an artist. If you are a one-person shop, you may play all of these roles. But if it's possible, don't prototype alone; find some game-loving co-workers to help you.

The following process should take you about two to three hours to do, excluding the initial preparation step. Don't try to make this perfect—it won't be. It's more important to get started and refine it over time. Good game design is an iterative process.

Step 1: Prepare for the Session

Before the team convenes to start prototyping, make sure you have the needed prototyping supplies:

- **Plenty of paper.** If you are prototyping a digital solution, use grid paper designed for the specific platform you are designing for (Figure 8-3). Flipchart paper works nicely for brainstorming and sketching early ideas and is about the right size for a board game.
- **Crayons, markers, or colored pencils.** Using something you can color with is extremely useful. Black and blue pens or gray pencils will do in a pinch,

but color enables you to distinguish between various parts of a game board or buttons on a screen more easily.

- **Scissors and tape.** You can use glue, but tape lends itself more to moving an item if you don't like its location.
- **Sticky notes.** Because they come in a variety of sizes and colors, sticky notes are highly versatile during prototyping. They are helpful for revealing information if you create a matching game or to stick on a die if you want to take turns by colors instead of by numbers.
- **Game items, such as dice, tokens, chips, and game markers.** You can easily and cheaply purchase these items from a game supply store or online. If you opt to purchase online, search for suppliers by using the phrase "supplies for making games." Alternatively, you can raid your existing supply of commercial games or office supplies for items you can use.
- **Initial design document,** with your instructional goal, learning objectives, player persona, and any constraints you need to factor into your design. The game design document should also specify the type of game you are creating: a tabletop game (board, dice, cards), a computer game (desktop, laptop, or tablet device), or a mobile game (smartphone). When you come to the prototyping session, you do not want to be discussing whether you are creating a tabletop game or a computer game.
- **Representative content** that supports the learning objectives you want to prototype.

For your prototyping session to be productive, you must bring bona fide learning content that supports the learning objectives you defined. Table 8-1 gives two examples of learning objectives you might design a game to achieve. You do not need exhaustive content—for example, you don't need to know every customer objection or every sales scenario in which it might crop up—but you do need representative content. You want enough content to play through one round or iteration of the game. Play-testers have to be able to experience all the elements of the game you are creating with learning content.

Table 8-1. Examples of Content You'll Need for a Useful Prototype

Learning Objective	Minimal Content Needed for Game Prototyping
Sales reps at Medical Devices Inc. can effectively respond to customer objections related to Product X.	• Three to four examples of real or realistic customer objections and the context in which those objections might occur. • Realistic distracters (wrong choices) for each example.
Employees at Retail Wonderland can implement a six-step customer service process while assisting customers.	• Description of process. • Three to four examples of typical customer interactions. • Common mistakes or pain points in the process.

In the examples listed in the table, if you try to prototype without content, you won't be able to verify whether your game idea will work with the content that needs to be included and whether it will help people learn what you need them to learn. You will face the same problem whatever your topic and objectives are. Without learning content, you risk designing a neat concept and loving it, only to find out in development that the actual learning content renders your great idea boring and ineffective.

Step 2: Brainstorm a Game Goal and Core Dynamic

Once the team gathers, start by reviewing the learning objectives you want to achieve with the game. Then brainstorm a potential game goal: Decide what challenge you want players to overcome or goal to achieve. Then decide what they will have to do to achieve that goal or overcome that challenge—that's the core dynamic of your game. The core dynamic works best when it supports the cognitive task or work behavior you want players to perform.

Here are some core dynamics that work well with learning games and align with common cognitive learning goals encountered in most organizations. (See chapter 1 for the additional core dynamics.)

- **Race to the finish.** This core dynamic cultivates competition, so avoid it if you want to encourage collaborative or cooperative work behavior.
- **Alignment.** If you have learning objectives related to learning or executing a process, this core dynamic is a good option.
- **Collection.** Collection can support knowledge and recall objectives as well as higher-order thinking objectives such as applying, analyzing, and evaluating. This core dynamic is effective if your objectives include the verbs *choose, interpret,* or *analyze.*
- **Exploration.** Exploration is usually coupled with another dynamic, such as collection or race to the finish. By itself, it may not achieve a learning objective, but it works great in conjunction with another dynamic that does support an objective. For example, your objective might include choose, interpret, or analyze. Exploration alone doesn't enable players to achieve those objectives, but exploration coupled with collection does. Players explore a variety of options and then choose something. If they choose correctly, they collect an item that they need.

Avoid spending more than about 20 minutes deciding on a game goal and a core dynamic. You can refine them as you execute other steps in this process. The key is to make a decision and start.

Step 3: Choose a Theme or Story

Once you have the idea for a game goal, you may find that a theme or story emerges at the same time. This theme or story should support your game's goal and, perhaps, the learning goal. Often, they flow together. Other times, you may not really have a theme or story you want to employ. For example, Scrabble has no overarching theme or story, but it works well as a game. The challenge of making words is sufficient.

Choosing a theme or story often makes everything else about the game design and prototyping process easier. It can help guide your decisions on game rules, aesthetics, and elements. A theme can also help players better understand the context in which the rules and learning of the game are to be applied. For example, when we opted to participate in an event focused on discussion of serious community issues, we wanted to explore the issue of homelessness. We ended up with a theme of "being a paycheck away," which drove many other game decisions. It helped us define the characters, issues they faced, and decisions they would need to make.

Step 4: Build a Physical Prototype

With a game goal, a core dynamic, and a theme in hand, you can start constructing a physical prototype of your game. Build your prototype to scale as much as you can. If you are designing a tabletop game, consider how big your game board, game cards, or other components will be. If you are designing a game for a smartphone, size your initial prototype to match the smallest phone you believe a player might use.

As you build, you will discover that deciding on rules and choosing game elements happens organically. Your big challenge is to stay focused on your learning objectives and ensure that game mechanics and elements align well—or at least do not conflict—with your objectives. You don't want to incorporate chance, for example, if it's not a part of the real-world context in which players would apply what they are learning in the game. If time or budget is a real-world constraint, figure out how to add game elements or rules that emulate this reality.

How the Game Goal, Core Dynamic, and Theme Come Together During Prototyping

In the board game A Paycheck Away, we wanted to help players emotionally identify with the challenges of being homeless: what it's like to be perilously close to it or struggling to get past it. We didn't need a theme, but we did need a story. In our initial prototyping story, we spent about 20 minutes crafting basic personas for six characters who were either homeless when the game begins or a paycheck away from being homeless. Once we had those personas locked in, it became easy to define some of the rules and game elements:

- **Job cards.** After we defined the characters in the game, we could easily identify the types of jobs they could reasonably apply for given their experience and education. We came up with jobs such as truck driver, server, bank teller, cashier, or warehouse worker.

- **Income guidelines.** Once we figured out possible jobs, it was easy to assign probable wages for those jobs. For example, the character of Willa worked as a cashier at a convenience store for 30 hours a week (so her employer wouldn't be required to pay benefits to her). Willa's probable wage is minimum wage, so it was easy to see that her family income was $220 a week or $880 a month.

- **Cash from paychecks, a township trustee, or other sources.** All players started with a certain amount of money, based on whether they had a job, had any savings, or were receiving some form of government assistance.

- **Chance, in the form of dice rolls and random events.** Once we knew our characters, we included chance cards that revealed events that would likely happen to them, such as a child getting sick, a car breaking down, availability of a food pantry, or a wallet being found. We also represented the challenges of finding housing or getting a job by using a die roll. If multiple players wanted the same job, they had to roll dice to see who got the job, with the player rolling the highest number getting the job.

- **Housing options, in the form of rules.** Players who had sufficient funds available could get Section 8 housing or rent a room in a pay-by-the week motel. Players without such funds either lived on the street or got space in a homeless shelter. However, the homeless shelter is usually only an option for 30 days' time. After that, players had to roll a die to see if they could remain in the shelter.

- **Other relevant rules.** Other rules to simulate real-world constraints faced by people who are a paycheck away or already homeless included the difficulty in affording childcare, the limited availability of substance abuse treatment programs, and the need to find housing that is on a bus line or accessible by another form of public transit.

- **Collaboration.** We made this a cooperative game as opposed to a competitive one. Instead of pitting players against one another, we chose to have players all working together to help one another out of homelessness. This decision involved players in all the characters' lives and stories.

Step 5: Play-Test and Revise Your Prototype

A good prototype enables someone to test the game play experience. Therefore, it must be more than sketches of a screen or a game board—it must be playable. Turn back to Figure 8-3, the prototype for the mobile game Mad Scientist. Note the working parts we created and taped together to simulate how players would add items to their cauldron, set the game level, and so on. These aspects of the prototype helped game testers get an idea of what actual game play would be like and how interactions would work. Static drawings do not do this. You may find it easier to first sketch a few screens to get an idea of the concept in front of everyone, but then shift to building a working prototype so you have something you can actually test.

Chapter 9 discusses the play-testing process in detail as you begin to involve others in testing your ideas. This first play-test of your prototype is the one you do within your team before even asking others to evaluate your idea. In this internal first test, you want to do the following:

- If your prototype is for a tabletop game, make sure the game board or cards include physical items the players will be interacting with in the game. This might be spaces on a game board, or specific kinds of game cards such as chance cards or opportunity cards.

- If your prototype is for a digital game, make sure your prototype reflects the actions players will make. If they need to tap "Play," for example, to initiate action, make sure you have a "Play" button included in your prototype. If they need to swipe left or right to make something move or to choose an option, you need to figure out how to represent this swipe on the prototype's "screen" to verify that players understand what you want them to do. If tapping on a section of the screen brings up a new set of options, your prototype needs to mimic that action.

- Make sure you document your initial set of game mechanics. If yours is a tabletop game, you need to write down the game mechanics so testers can read them before playing. If yours is a digital game, you need to convey rules by actions players can take or messages, cues, or tutorials you embed within the game.

- Make sure the learning content works well with the core dynamic and game elements you've selected.

- Agree, at least within your team, on how engaging playing the prototype seems to be. If your team is not enjoying it, odds are your external players won't either.

After play-testing your paper prototype, make any revisions you think are necessary before you invite others to play. This might mean tweaking rules. It might mean adding extra spaces on a game board. It might mean drawing a few new screens on a digital prototype or creating a couple of buttons you hadn't thought about.

How Prototyping Differs With Digital Games

These five steps outline a process you can use for either tabletop games or digital ones. However, you'll want to keep a few other elements in mind as you craft digital prototypes:

- You may have lots of little pieces you use to simulate actions a player makes in your digital games. You may need to create icons, buttons, sliders, and so on. You may also need to consider special pop-up screens that appear if a player does something incorrectly or a prompt that appears if a player can't figure out what to do next. Obviously you don't have this kind of system interaction with a tabletop game.

- Digital games often include a tutorial on how to play, in lieu of a set of rules that players might read when playing a tabletop game. While you might document your game rules as part of prototyping a tabletop game, you will not create a tutorial as part of your first prototype of your digital game. That's because subsequent play-testing with typical players helps you figure out what your tutorial needs to include—and what you can alter in your design to eliminate the need for overly detailed tutorials. You will want players to intuitively figure out what to tap, select, or swipe.

- Digital prototypes usually involve a two-step process: You prototype on paper first, and then you shift to a digital prototyping tool. You may also want to do some preliminary sketches of your idea before you start building the prototype. These initial sketches can be helpful, but they are not a replacement for a functional prototype that people can actually test. This intermediate step is a nice bridge to development. It enables you to input some simple graphics and simulate progression in the game.

Work on Your Own

Prototyping is best learned by doing. With that in mind, here's a design exercise you can try with some of your teammates. You might not think you're ready for this task yet; however, we've found that the best way to start developing a learning game is to simply begin. The best way to learn is to start designing a prototype. You can use the template in appendix 5 as you work.

Your Task

Create and play-test a learning game. Choose to create either a tabletop game or a digital game for a tablet or smartphone. Allocate about 2.5 hours to complete the task.

Game Background

- **Game topic:** Build a culture that drives customer loyalty.
- **Organization you are making it for:** A local pizzeria that distinguishes itself from competitors by trying to make the experience amazing from the time a customer places an order to the time the customer pays the bill.
- **Target audience:** The waitstaff who are your frontline customer service providers, typically college-aged, with most attending the local university and working part time.
- **Instructional goal:** When interacting with customers on the job, waitstaff will display an attitude that customers love and consistently make small gestures

that show they are attentive to customers. They will find ways to surprise and delight every customer at some point during the dining experience. The learning objectives are:

- Distinguish between customer satisfaction and customer loyalty, and define both from the customer's perspective.
- Avoid common mistakes and figure out strategies for avoiding them.
- Identify and incorporate a variety of loyalty-building behaviors into the process of waiting on a customer.

Possible content to incorporate into your prototype:

Behaviors That Satisfy	Behaviors That Drive Loyalty	Common Mistakes to Avoid
• Knowing the product • Getting the order right	• Exuding a consistently great attitude • Making small gestures that show you notice the customer • Going beyond what's expected to what surprises and delights	• Failing to smile, make eye contact, and pay attention to your customers throughout their dining experience • Being unprepared—for example, not knowing the daily specials and being unfamiliar with the menu • Not writing the order down; not repeating the order back • Doing what's expected, but not what is memorable

Process to Use

1. Choose a game goal.
2. Select one or two of the dynamics below. Your game goal largely dictates which of these you choose:
   - **Race to the finish.** Players might compete against one another or against a timer to serve the most customers.
   - **Territory acquisition.** Players might need to acquire territory—tables within the restaurant—by demonstrating the proper customer service mentality.
   - **Escape or rescue.** Players might need to free customers from some trap with their exemplary service skills.
   - **Collection.** Players might collect tips in a jar, based on how they perform in the game. The player with the most tips at the end wins.
   - **Alignment.** Players might need to fill all the tables in a specified order.
3. Determine if you want to include a theme or a story.
4. Decide whether the game will be cooperative, competitive, or a blend of the two.
5. Create a paper prototype of that game. Define your game mechanics (rules

of the game, how you move, how you acquire territory, and so on) as you go. Consider game elements to include (resources, rewards, strategy, chance, and so on).

6. Play-test. (See chapter 9 for details on how to do a phase 1 prototype.)

To create this challenge, we modified one of the processes in *Challenges for Game Designers* (2009), by Brenda Brathwaite and Ian Schreiber. The customer service scenario is our own. If you want to further your practice in game design, *Challenges for Game Designers* can be a great place to get ideas.

Wrap-Up

Prototyping saves time and gives you that first quick test of your game idea. For learning games, you must incorporate learning content in the prototype. Otherwise, you cannot test the effectiveness of your game prototype in helping people learn what you want them to learn. You may find yourself refining your ideas on paper several times before you move into development. Time spent with paper typically saves you time and money later. The next chapter will walk you through how to play-test your prototype.

Play-Testing

In This Chapter

✓ What's a play-test and how do I do one?
✓ What kinds of play-tests should you conduct?
✓ How do you collect and analyze feedback during play-testing?
✓ Examples of iteration in game designs (initial prototype, second version, final version)
✓ Work on your own
✓ Guru game play opportunity

No matter how much design and care you put into creating your game, and no matter how much you play it, the real feedback and insights occur when other people play it. Inevitably, they will find game irregularities, mistakes, and leaps in logic that you didn't notice. As a result, one of the most important steps in designing a learning game is to conduct multiple play-tests. Figure 9-1 shows you where we are in the game design process.

Figure 9-1. Learning-Game Design Process: Play-Test

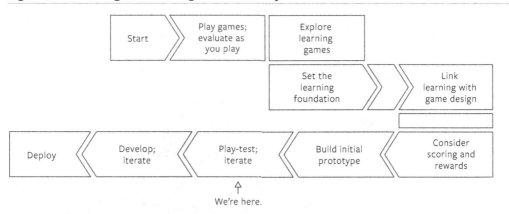

At a high level, play-testing is not usability testing, focus group testing, quality assurance testing, or internal design review. It is "playability" testing. You are testing how the game experience "feels" to the players. Does the game make sense? Is it easy to understand how to play? Are the rules easy to follow? Are the players engaged? Is it not too hard, but not too easy? Is it complete? Do players learn what they should learn by playing the game? Play-testing is what you do to refine and craft your game to the point where it performs as you intended—as a game and as a learning solution.

Successfully developing a learning game is an iterative process. Likewise, play-testing is not something you do once or twice. You do it several times, each test further refining the game play and learning experience. For a small learning game (simple board game or a small mini game), you should assume four to six hours of play-testing time per person who play-tests. For a bigger game (more complex board game or a full-scale mobile or digital game), assume 10 to 40 hours of testing per person, at a minimum. For large games such as *Halo* or *The Sims,* designers may have done up to 3,000 hours of play-testing to verify that their game worked. Because you should aim to involve between four and six play-testers, you can assume a minimum of 16 hours—going all the way up to 120 hours—of play-testing.

Play-Test Phases

You should plan to go through three major phases of play-testing. The first phase begins with the first version of the learning game you create—your paper prototype. The second phase involves play-testing with people outside the design team. The third and final phase will be with a game that looks almost finished. Each phase involves multiple rounds of play-testing.

Your biggest risk is to play-test too little. During the entire process, you want to discover what works and where the holes are. So the more you play-test, the cleaner and more refined your final game will be. Let's look at what should happen in each phase of testing.

1. Concept Test

During the early phase of play-testing, you and your design team play the initial prototype and evaluate it (Figure 9-2). Now is the time to discuss and work with the game to improve the initial design. As you play, allow and encourage modifying the game mechanics and elements on the fly. You should keep game materials basic for this test, ideally using paper.

Figure 9-2. First Play-Test of a Mobile Game

When play concludes, have all players rate the experience and suggest enhancements and changes. Document any decisions you make to alter aspects of the game. If your game is digital, you might decide to create a digital prototype and then do this type of play-test again before you invest in any actual programming.

2. Play Test With Those Outside Your Team

Before testing your game with outsiders, play it again as an internal team to verify that your changes during phase 1 worked as planned. Once you decide the game is up to your standards as a design team, move to phase 2 testing and pull in perspectives outside your team. Your outside group should include five or six people who represent your target players. Relying on a single representative can be risky: With only one true target player, you will find it difficult to discern if this person's feedback is sufficient to represent feedback typical of most members. However, with five or six people, as long as they are representative, you can uncover a majority of the issues (Nielsen 2000). If you are doing this game for a client within or outside your organization, you need to include the client-side project manager or stakeholder.

During phase 2 testing, your game assets should be some reasonable version of what you anticipate final game components will look like, but the game is likely to still have rough edges to it. (For a digital game, you won't likely have a fully finished version ready.) You should seek input on aesthetics, game rules, scoring, and complexity, as well as the learning value of various activities. You probably won't have all levels built because you are still gathering feedback that will inform design decisions. And you probably won't have all game aesthetics or rules in place, but you should have enough for players to give meaningful feedback on the overall play and learning experiences (Figure 9-3).

Figure 9-3. Play-Testing a Learning Game

Finally, phase 2 testing needs to be more structured and formal than phase 1. You should schedule the play-test and have an agenda with timeframes for setting up the format and guidelines for testing, playing the game, and conducting a post-play debrief. Later, this chapter outlines a process for executing this kind of play-test and questions to ask during the debriefing.

3. Beta Play-Test With Target Audience

Beta testing may involve several iterations of your game, or only one. The number of beta tests you do depends on the scope and complexity of your game. For a simple tabletop game, this phase may mean a pilot session of whatever learning solution is incorporating your game. For a digital game, you may need several iterations before you get to a final one, and you may extend testing to dozens of players to simulate a variety of browsers, devices, and other technical aspects.

At this point, your testers should fully reflect your target learners—not friendly co-workers. You want these testers to be unquestionably objective. This play-test group should represent people who really need to learn the content within your game. Otherwise, the testers may rate your game lower simply because it's not of interest or relevance to them.

The beta test should be performed on an almost-complete game; it should look like a full-fledged game with no missing features. You want the players focused on playing and not on game pieces, graphics, or other minor distractions. You may still have small unfinished elements as you await final feedback, but the game should be nearly finished.

But you can be clever about beta testing even if every piece of development or programming is not quite done. For example, Karl oversaw the development of a complex game created in the software Unity, which allows for 3-D animation and interaction. Fully programming the tutorial before final feedback would have been costly if major changes that would affect the opening tutorial ended up being needed. Instead, Karl's team created a tutorial with a simple PowerPoint slide deck with branching capabilities. The tutorial described the navigation without the need to have it programmed using screen captures. The team then incorporated suggested changes to the PowerPoint tutorial into the finished tutorial.

After the play experience, you want to debrief and then decide what changes to make. By this time, you will have invested substantial time and effort into the game design and development. So you may not be as open to some suggestions as you should be at this point. On the other hand, be careful to distinguish between minor or inconsequential adjustments and suggestions that will make a real difference. Most important, make sure the game accomplishes the learning goals and provides the outcomes you desire.

Framing the Play-Test for the Testers

When administering a play-test at any phase, here are some good guidelines to keep in mind:

- Tell testers who the typical user of the game will be and convey any relevant background about what they should already know or know how to do. Give them enough context so they understand how and where the game will be used.
- Don't share any information before people play unless you plan to share this same information with actual players in the same manner. That's part of the play-test. Can your players "get it" without you explaining what the game is about?
- Tell them what to expect. For example, "This game will last 15-20 minutes, and then will be followed by a Q&A."
- Emphasize the need for play-testers to think out loud as they play. You want to hear their internal thoughts spoken aloud—for example, "This is really confusing," "I don't understand the rules," and "I wonder what would happen if I make this choice?" are all helpful thoughts for play-testers to say aloud.
- Take a backseat during the play-test, and stay silent as much as you can. Do help players if they truly are stuck, but try to limit your interactions with players during the game. If you have to help players, make a note of where you have to so you can address it as part of creating the next iteration of the game.
- Stop play after about 20 minutes and conclude with debrief questions.
- Keep a play-testing journal or log that documents the results of each play-test you do and chronicles the decisions you make about game changes.

Collecting Feedback

During the play-testing process, you collect data and determine what works and what needs to be tweaked. A systematic, driven decision-making process helps you avoid adjusting the game based on one person's opinion or preference.

Here are four ways to collect data from a play-test. Even though some of the following processes are opinion-based, collecting opinions from multiple people helps identify real issues. Hearing the same comment repeatedly might suggest a critical issue. Also pay attention to comments that validate concerns you had when you began the testing process.

Observation

Watching players interact with the game space and the rules of the game is critical. In a paper prototype, you can witness confusion or uncertainty among players, as well as how they interpret the rules or move about the game. If your game is multiplayer, you can see how players interact with one another and how this affects game play and learning.

With digital games, several software tools can track key strokes or the time a player spends hovering over a button or a particular area, and even provide a heat map of where the player ventured within the game. This is especially useful for phase 2 play-testing. These types of software programs can be helpful for tracking what a player decides to do within a game and showcasing points where a player gets confused by directions, navigation, or user interface design. UserTesting.com is one example of a site that enables you to test a digital app or web experience. Testing done on this site lets you specify the number of testers you want, the specific tasks you want testers to perform, and any post-test questions you want to pose. You receive a video that enables you to watch exactly what testers did and how they reacted to your game.

Think Aloud

While observation is great for determining where players went within a game and what they did within it, it can't tell you what they were thinking. In early play-testing especially, you want to combine observation with a request that players think aloud as they play. Since player impressions and emotions are important in the design and playing of learning games, it's helpful to know what players are thinking as they participate in the game.

The think aloud technique is simple. Players articulate at every stage of the game what they are thinking. For example, a player may read a rule and then say, "This rule makes sense to me because it explains what to do if I roll two of the same numbers," or "I'm confused. I don't know what to do next." As players think aloud, your job is to capture this feedback. If they get too quiet, your job is to remind them to continue to think aloud. Their insights can help you modify the game and make it more effective. Plus you'll find out if what you intended to occur within the play space actually happens.

Much of the software that allows online usability testing permits the testers to record themselves playing and thinking aloud as they execute the tasks your test specifies. By watching and listening to the recordings, you can identify points of confusion in your game and find out what the player likes or dislikes.

Post-Play-Test Interviews

Asking people to reflect on their game play and learning experience either verbally or in writing is a good way to obtain information about the experience in a thoughtful manner. While a think aloud happens as the player experiences the game, an interview occurs after the game, when the design team asks players to answer questions related to the experience and what they learned by playing the game. This works best when guided by a series of targeted questions (see later in the chapter for question samples). You can then codify answers and review them to determine common themes. The interview also provides a chance to dig a little deeper into the impressions and experience in the game.

Pre/Post-Testing

You create a learning game to help people learn, yet game designers often gloss over assessing how effectively people learn during play-testing. In addition to asking players what they learned in the post-play-test interview, gather more concrete evidence of what they learned. You can test learning with a baseline test before the players engage with the game and then administer a test once they finish. This provides a method of measuring learning gains.

Analyzing Play-Test Results

Regardless of how you collect data during your play-test, it's important to carefully analyze what you gather. In game development, you can easily get caught up with your own game design and cringe whenever another person criticizes what you've developed. Instead, you need to take the feedback and establish processes to make the necessary adjustments. This starts with quantifying the data as much as possible. Use a five- or seven-point scale for reactions, code answers, and, if possible, record players' reactions so you can come back and objectively review what happened at certain points in the game. If you plan to use a point scale, agree on an acceptable score before you play-test. For example, we usually want players to rate a game as at least a 4 out of 5 in terms of how engaged they felt with the experience. If our average across play-testers is less than this and our most common rating (mode) doesn't reach this level, we know we have to continue to work on the game to improve its engagement factor.

While testers' comments are a rich source of feedback, not all feedback is equally valid. Designing a learning game and adjusting the game based on feedback is as much an art as it is a science. You need to weigh testers' comments in the context of both the players' experience and the desired goals of the team and stakeholders. You also have to weigh them against other changes you may have already made from a previous round of play-testing. For example, you may have specifically added a rule to better achieve a particular learning outcome that wasn't met in previous versions of the game. Play-testing clearly shows you the rule works, but what if an individual tester tells you she doesn't like the rule? Well, if the rule provides you with the desired outcome, you may choose to ignore that particular piece of feedback. The cost of doing additional tweaking may not be worth the time investment in continuing to explore other options for achieving your result.

So when do you make a change and when do you keep something as-is? This is a key aspect of analyzing play-test results. Is a comment from a single play-tester not worth listening to, or does it include a grain of truth? As the game designer, you will need to decide which feedback to take to heart and which to ignore. Here are three examples of feedback to act on:

- You have consensus from all play-testers that a game element or mechanic is not working. A consensus is usually a good opportunity for a second look at something possibly amiss in the game.
- Your overarching score averages on a particular element—such as engagement, learning value, clarity of play, and balance—are lower than you want.
- You observe a player doing something unintended that has a major impact on the game's effectiveness as a learning experience. Because you may only have four to six people testing, if a major unintended event occurs, it's worth retesting to see if you can replicate this unintended event or making a change to preclude it happening again. For example, perhaps one person completely missed the instructions for what to do in an online game. Missing these instructions

caused a fail state that generates a false report on competency with the learning materials. It may be worth figuring out how to make instructions clearer—or forcing a tutorial before allowing play—to prevent people from failing due to lack of expertise with game play as opposed to knowledge of learning material.

Questions to Ask Play-Testers

Naturally, when we think about play-test interviews and feedback, we want to think about what questions will obtain the desired data to improve the game. While it is tempting to create a giant list of questions to ask in a play-test, the following questions provide a good deal of constructive feedback that can be used to inform future iterations of your game.

What one word best describes your game play experience? This question provides a quick assessment of the experience while forcing the player to condense the entire experience into a single expression. The condensation of the experience can provide you with information related to the player's overall feelings and experiences. Look at answers clustered around a certain word or concept and compare those clusters with your desired outcomes. If they are far from one another, you will need to reconfigure the experience.

What did you learn? This question can elicit what players think they've learned from the game. Compare responses with what people were supposed to learn. If people didn't learn, the game hasn't worked, no matter how engaging or awesome players think it was. It's critical you get people to tell you what they learned in their own words so you can compare it against the learning goal and learning objectives of the game and any pre- and post-test data you obtain. You can also provide the learning goals and ask the players to rate how effective they believe the game was in helping them reach those goals. Consider using a 1-5 scale, with 1 being low and 5 being high.

How engaging was the game? To get to the bottom of this question, ask the players to rate on a scale of 1-5 their engagement level in the game. This is important because if players aren't engaged, it's hard for them to learn, negating the value of learning games. During game play, you don't want a player to mentally check out and not learn much of anything.

Did your engagement level change at any point during play (increase or decrease)? If it did change, why? You will want to know if players' level of engagement changed at any time. Engagement levels naturally fluctuate, so it's not immediately a bad sign, but as the designer, you need to know when those changes occur. For example, there could be a confusing game element, a rule that needs to be changed or enhanced, or some other part of the game that requires adjustment to maximize the experience. Conversely, the game could start slow but then build in excitement for players. You want to assess all of this and determine if and how you should tweak the game goal, the core dynamic, the game mechanics, or the game elements. Careful listening and data analysis can help you decide if you need to adjust a game element, a rule, or even the game's goal or core dynamic.

What, if anything, did you find confusing or hard to understand as you played? Encourage play-testers to explain their responses. You want to know if the rules were clear and realistic to learn. So don't accept a simple, "The rules were confusing"; you want more detailed information. Even with a good game, there can be some confusion about how to play. Your job is to figure out whether players' confusion warrants action on your part. Did their confusion affect their learning or engagement? If not, you may decide to do nothing. Was confusion limited to a single player, or did many players report the same confusion? This is good information to compare with the think aloud activity. Find out if the learners remembered where they became stuck or frustrated. You may also want to ask the learners if they would suggest adding any other rules or even eliminating ones that didn't make sense to them or improve the game.

What, in your words, was the learning objective of the game? The response to this question can be telling. If play-testers respond with an objective too far removed from the actual learning objective, you may need to dramatically change the design of the game.

What information do you wish you had when playing the game? Sometimes the designers of a learning game become so wrapped up in the process that they take certain things for granted, such as assumed prerequisite knowledge. This question can also help identify any missing information in the rules or description of how to play the game.

Was there anything you didn't like about the game? What was it? Most likely you aren't going to change your entire game because someone doesn't like a particular part of the game. However, pointing out the pain points or flaws in a game before its release beyond the play-test groups can help you avoid larger problems and provides you with time to mediate elements that might not be enjoyed by large groups of players.

Play-Testing in Action

Let's look at how A Paycheck Away evolved based on the play-testing phases outlined earlier in this chapter. In this example, the game had four rounds of play-testing from start to finish. In each round, we added progressively more people to the play-testing process. More information is shared on this game in chapter 11 as part of showcasing implementation strategies that maximize success of your learning game.

1. Test the Prototype

The game's learning goal was to help people learn the speed with which working people can become homeless, and the challenges of getting out of that situation. To win, all players had to be in permanent housing after three months elapsed in the game. The original game play was designed so that each player took a turn in each imaginary "week" of the game (12 weeks total). This turned out to be a lot of turns within the game. Our play-test enabled us to identify this as a problem.

As shown in Figure 9-4, we created the first prototype on 8½ × 11 paper. Our game components included a game board made with PowerPoint and role-playing sheets and game cards made in Word, along with money borrowed from a Monopoly game to serve as our cash for players.

Figure 9-4. Initial Prototype for A Paycheck Away

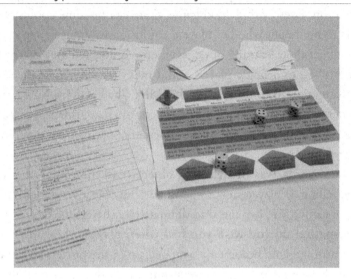

Our initial play-test was with the four people who were the game design team members. We played for about 20 minutes, discussing ideas as we went. We then debriefed and brainstormed changes to make for the next iteration, which would include graphics and appropriately sized game components (Figure 9-5).

Figure 9-5. An Interim Version of A Paycheck Away

Here are four examples of what we learned and modified based on our initial play-test:

- **The game play lasted too long, and people were bored unless it was their turn.** The initial rule for how people took turns was the problem. Our solution was to have all players involved during each turn and for each player's turn to move everyone forward by a week in the month. After four turns, players would be at the end of a month of homelessness or near-homelessness, depending on what role they had.

- **Tracking payments mentally was too hard, and having to do this task weekly consumed too much time.** In the game, money changes hands frequently, and players constantly have to pay bills. Our solution for tracking was to include a budget sheet that players use to track income and expenses as they go. To reduce time involved in tracking payments, we shifted to paying people twice in a month rather than weekly.

- **If multiple players wanted a job, we only wanted one of them to be able to get it.** This mirrors real-world constraints. Our solution was to incorporate a die roll, with the highest die roll getting the job.

- **We needed a way to show how variable the income from food-server jobs can be and for people to quickly calculate how much they'd made in a two-week period.** We paid out wages in the game every two weeks and had people pay bills every two weeks as well. Our solution was to have people roll dice to figure out what tips they'd earned. The varying rolls would show the highs and lows over time of income based on tips.

2. Have Fellow Employees Play the Game

In the next round of play-testing, we invited employees of Bottom-Line Performance who were not part of the design team to play and give feedback. We printed a tiled version of a game board and taped it together. We observed them playing and conducted a post-play-test interview with them. We made additional tweaks to the rules to increase clarity; there was a lot of confusion over payments as well as who could do things based on a chance card or job card being drawn. We recognized the need for the "game master" role to have a clear game master guide to refer to during game play. We also got feedback from players that the organization of the game board was a bit confusing and made it hard for them to figure out where to put their tokens.

3. Bring In the Strangers

After we modified the game again, it was time to invite strangers to test the game. We invited members of the Central Indiana Chapter of the Association for Talent Development to play-test. We had 15 play-testers spread across three groups. Members of the design team each observed a single group. The team lead, Sharon, then did a focus-group-style debrief with a predefined set of questions. Because of the large number of play-testers, we handled the interview in round-robin fashion. We asked each person to give a numerical ranking on engagement and elaborate on the rationale of the ranking. As we moved on, the next person gave a ranking. If the tester agreed with the rationale of the previous tester, he simply indicated agreement. If he had a unique comment to share, he added it.

People's feedback was overwhelmingly positive, but we still had changes to make. One example was how we presented all the game roles to players. Players had a sheet that explained what role they would play and key facts about that role. At the game's start, players introduced themselves in character and shared their backstory. As game play progressed, however, players found it tough to recall all the key facts about each role and spent time during game play hunting for the info on the role sheets. Our solution was to create two-sided name tents that summarized key info—name, situation, income, and challenges. All players could easily read the info. Problem solved.

4. The Final Version

Figure 9-6 shows an image from the event during which we launched A Paycheck Away. The game included polished game components: a game board, role sheets, money, tokens, role tents, and game cards. Printing costs—while discounted because we designed the game pro bono for Dayspring Center, a homeless shelter—still exceeded $1,500. Play-testing with inexpensively printed materials saved a lot of money. Previous rounds of play-testing also ensured a terrific play and learning experience for the 150 players who showed up to play the game at the event.

Figure 9-6. Playing the Finished Version

Work on Your Own

Conducting a play-test is an important process when creating a learning game. After you complete the game design prototype activity outlined in the last chapter, take this opportunity to conduct a play-test.

Select a group of four to six individuals to conduct a play-test. You can use the worksheet in appendix 7 to guide feedback, or you can create your own feedback sheet to gather the information you think will be of the most benefit in shaping your game.

Guru Game Play Opportunity

To reinforce your knowledge of play-testing, go to Game Design Guru and try the play-testing level. In no time, you'll be able to demonstrate your knowledge of play-testing. Remember, go to www.theknowledgeguru.com/ATDGameDesignGuru and play to learn!

Wrap-Up

This chapter walked you through the process of play-testing your game from start to finish. Play-testing is critical to developing an effective learning game. The time you spend in play-testing will directly translate into learning outcomes and helps ensure that your game will meet the desired outcomes. Your next step in the process of designing a learning game is to move from design to development. In some cases, there will be a little overlap because the play-testing is iterative. The next chapter will discuss the types of tools that can help you create your finished learning game.

Part 4

Development and Implementation

Development Considerations

In This Chapter

✓ Who should make up your development team?
✓ What tools are available to assist with development?
✓ Will the Agile methodology work for game design?
✓ With a limited budget, how can you work with external resources?

We have waited until chapter 10 to discuss what is needed to develop a game from a technical standpoint, but don't let that be an indication of when you need to start thinking about development (Figure 10-1 shows you where you are in the process.) From the very first design meeting, you need to be thinking forward to your game's eventual development. Depending on the type of game you hope to develop (tabletop or digital), the tools you may need range from Microsoft Office to Adobe tools to a sophisticated game engine.

Figure 10-1. Learning-Game Design Process: Development

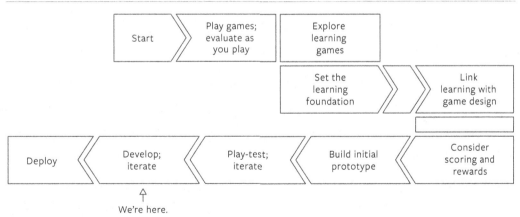

Wouldn't it be great to create a paper prototype, design the exact pie-in-the-sky game that you want, and then find the right tool or team to develop your dream learning game? Unfortunately, that's not reality for most learning game designers. Instead, the game development budget and skills you have at your disposal, as well as technical constraints, dictate the type of game you create and how it gets developed. Given that reality, this chapter explores the tradeoffs and functionality of various game development tools. Read through the choices and then decide what budget and skill set you can allocate to your learning game.

Resource Needs and Considerations

Learning games require many roles, so they usually involve a team rather than a single person. If you can play multiple roles, you may be able to successfully design a tabletop game solo or create a smaller digital game housed within an e-learning authoring tool.

If your game is bigger in magnitude, needs high-end graphics or multiple levels, or is being deployed as a native app, you will need outside expertise. Even for early-stage game design, it's tough to go it alone. If you are a one-person team, consider seeking out people within your organization who enjoy playing games to help you with game design and testing. Chances are you'll be able to find people who play games at home, with friends, and maybe even on teams.

It is hard to be part of a development team if you are unfamiliar with different types of games. Having experienced gamers on your team makes the development process easier. Each round of play-testing you do typically results in altering some aspect of the game's design. Gamers can help evaluate outcomes of play-tests and devise solutions to problems the play-test reveals.

The key roles listed in Table 10-1 provide a good start for game projects of simple to medium complexity. Large-scale projects would have additional roles such as an overarching product owner, music technicians, and level designers.

On the client side, several roles should be involved as well, including the project sponsor, subject matter expert (SME), and IT liaison.

The project sponsor funds the project and serves as the ultimate decision maker, who signs off on the game's final version. As the game designer, you ensure the project sponsor knows what's happening.

Table 10-1. Roles and Responsibilities of Your Design Team

Role and Key Responsibilities	Mistakes to Avoid
Project Manager • Creates and monitors work plans for moving from design through development • Schedules and facilitates team meetings • Documents and communicates decisions and status • Monitors and communicates status; resolves issues that arise • Holds team members accountable for various deliverables and meeting target dates; negotiates changes and unanticipated challenges	• Assuming the role is a minor one • Assuming an inexperienced person can do this role • Allowing more features and functions to sneak into the game during development

Role and Key Responsibilities	Mistakes to Avoid
Instructional Designer or Writer • Works with the client to define the instructional goal and objectives for the overarching learning experience, which includes the game and other related curriculum • Identifies specific instructional objectives for the game • Determines the type and quantity of content that must be included to achieve the learning objectives • Works with the subject matter experts to gather information and write the game content • Checks the decisions included in game play to ensure that learning is the outcome • Develops pre- and post-tests	• Directing the game to be too content focused at the expense of game play experience • Turning the game into a learning activity instead of a game • Having too linear an approach to the game play
Game Designer • Ensures learning experience is a game, rather than some other type of learning activity • Helps choose appropriate game mechanics and game elements • Determines logical game scoring that is also aligned with learning needs • Adds insights into what makes a game engaging	• Focusing too much on entertainment value • Losing sight of learning outcomes • Developing overly complex scoring system • Developing hard-to-understand rules
Artist • Responsible for aesthetic look and feel of the game • Creates a visual theme that draws players into the game • Ensures consistency in the feel of the game • Creates the first impression players have of the game	• Spending too much time on art • Making the look more realistic than it needs to be for the game • Creating artwork that is hard to reproduce in print (if board or card game)
Programmer or Developer (for digital games) • Programs or authors game using appropriate software tools • Understands how the game is to function and the desired outcomes of the game from a technical standpoint • Communicates to the team about what is and is not possible given the allocated time and authoring tool	• Inadequately documenting code and variables • Failing to test effects of one change throughout entire game • Creating overly complex code • Thinking "the player will never do X" • Making mistakes in programming the scoring algorithm
Quality Assurance (for play-testing) • Checks on game flow and feel as well as features and functionality • Tests games after changes have been made to ensure it still functions as desired • Tests different facets of the game, such as scoring, navigation, and rules	• Failing to think like the final end user of the game • Failing to test in different browsers (if digital game) • Taking game rules for granted or making assumptions • Not having the right play-testers for the stage of the project you are in

The SME helps make sure that the game focuses on the content that players need to learn. Having more than one SME look at the game and contribute content may help you develop a truer picture of what needs to be learned. During development, SMEs should provide learning content you request as the instructional designer and verify the accuracy of content and any outcomes players experience as a result of decisions they make using this content. Ideally, the SME understands and plays games. If not, you can run into resistance and frustration. For example, one of the requirements a SME wanted for an online board game was that every player needed to land on every square of the board so no one would miss any content. Essentially, without the element of chance from a spinner or dice, there was no game, just a march from one square to another. What you want to avoid is letting SMEs provide too much content or too heavily influence game elements or mechanics, especially if they don't understand game design.

If you are developing a game that runs on any type of computer or mobile device outside your existing learning management system, you need to involve someone within your IT department as soon as possible. You need guidance and decisions on these issues before you can even formulate a game design:

- Do game scores need to be sent to a learning management system?
- Are plug-ins supported with the standard browser within your organization?
- If the game is a native app, does your organization have an enterprise account where the app can reside?
- What level of security audit does your solution have to pass through?
- Who will maintain the game post-launch, answer user support questions, and troubleshoot technical problems?
- Where will the final game reside—in the cloud or on your organization's servers? Will a single sign-on be required?

Development Tools

Finding the right development tool for your game can seem daunting. You can choose a simple template offered by many different suppliers, use a tool like PowerPoint, or leverage 3-D tools and programming languages such as Lua, C++, SQL, or Java. And, of course, there are dozens of options in between.

Understanding the various options can help guide your development efforts and provide you with a method of matching the right tool to the right type of project. Table 10-2 highlights the various tools and the games you can create with them. Be aware that with the exception of tools requiring no or low programming knowledge, the learning curve is significant. If you are doing a single game project and you want a high-end digital game, your better choice is to work with an external supplier who can do the development work on your behalf.

Table 10-2. Development Tools for Designing Your Game

Type of Tool	Types of Games	Degree of Programming Knowledge Needed	Sample Products	Notes
Office productivity software	Basic branching; text-based stories	None	PowerPoint; Word	Takes skill to create the exact type of result you want.
Templates	Matching games; question and answer games; simple drag and drop games	None	Raptivity; eLearning Brothers	Work well with games involving multiple-choice questions. There are tools for live classrooms as well.
Game-based platforms	Templated games with robust back ends and customization options	None	Axonify; Knowledge Guru	Bridge gap between low-complexity templates and complex game engines. Supports play across all devices.
Authoring and development tools	Branching; multiple choice games; drag and drop games	Medium	Captivate; Storyline products	Most basic elements are in these tools, but more sophisticated games require medium- to high-level skills.
Game creation software	Arcade-style games; side-scrollers	Medium	GameMaker Pro; Construct 2	Can create robust games if you have instructional design skills. The instructional design is not part of the tool's design.
Branching and simulation software	Sophisticated branching	Low to Medium	Twine; SimWriter	Good for multibranching simulations with high levels of choice.
Classroom audience response tools	In-class question-and-answer games; true or false	None	Kahoot!; Poll Everywhere	Good for question-and-answer games and getting immediate feedback from a class.
HTML5 tools	Sophisticated interactions; resource allocation games	High	JavaScript; Phaser	Need excellent programming skills to make this work.
3-D software	First-person-thinker games; immersive game environment	High	Torque 3D; Unreal Engine;	In addition to software skills, need to have 3-D modeling skills to create objects.

The Agile Methodology and Game Design

Regardless of the type of tool you use, you need a development methodology. One method frequently associated with game development is the Agile method (Figure 10-2). This method is often preferred because it allows for rapid iterations and changes to the game as you develop it.

Figure 10-2. An Agile Approach to Learning-Game Design

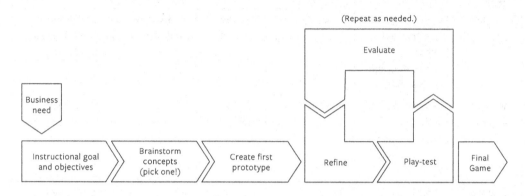

The Agile method has variations, but the process is essentially a series of "sprints." The end of each sprint, which usually spans one to four weeks, results in a working version of the game. The input to the process is the instructional goal and learning objectives, along with some relevant content to assist in prototyping. (Chapters 4 and 5 outlined this portion of the process; the Agile portion of the process usually begins with prototype development, described in chapter 7.) After you develop the prototype, your team refines and iterates, creating a new, more polished version of the game. The concept driving Agile development is that you don't refine the game design until it is perfect and then move to development. You keep iterating on the game's design as you develop it, until you reach a version that meets your instructional objectives and results in satisfactory learner engagement.

After the prototype process, you create a list of requirements that you think should be in the minimal viable version of the product, or MVP. The list is naturally incomplete because as you begin to develop and test the game, you discover more requirements that you need to add. Your team prioritizes the requirements, and then builds them into the next version as part of the following sprint. Once the period is over, you play-test the game again. You repeat this process until the game is ready to be developed. In fact, the Agile process is often used in the actual development of the game as well because games look and feel somewhat different as they evolve from the first paper prototype to the final version. However, by that time, the changes should not be dramatic and made to the underlying game mechanics or game elements. Each sprint ends with the "release" of a version of your game product. Each iteration has a bit more functionality and polish until you hit the final version of the game.

Three tools help keep an Agile project on schedule: a sprint schedule, a build list, and an error log.

Sprint Schedule

The Agile process usually starts with creating a schedule that outlines the work for each sprint at a high level. The sprint schedule provides information about what is to be developed, how long it will take to develop, the timeframe of the development effort, and the time commitments of such various contributors as the artist, developer, and owner of the task to be completed. In the table, time is shown as "points," with one point equating to a day's effort. For example, it will take five people approximately 5.75 days to complete the first task. They are not all working on it full time, and the table indicates the exact time commitment of each person.

For the sake of brevity, Table 10-3 shows just one sprint. Multiple sprints are usually required to reach a final version.

Our intent is not to teach you Agile development, but rather encourage you to adopt a few of its primary concepts and tools. The main benefit of Agile development is its focus on small iterations and the concept of "protecting a sprint": not adding new work into a sprint once it begins. This keeps your project moving and allows for frequent testing as you go along. The end product tends to be better and the entire process is more efficient.

If you get into developing a larger game, use Agile software created specifically to help with the process. If you don't, you may want to create a build list using word processing or spreadsheet software. The build list is the translation of the sprint schedule into discrete tasks. It is a tool used to identify each task to be completed by an individual in a sprint.

Build List

Keep in mind that to keep the sprint moving, you should not make changes to the build list during the sprint (Table 10-4). Instead, you should discuss changes and make them before the next sprint. If you allow changes during the sprint, chaos can ensue.

Error Log

Once a sprint is complete, you'll want to have people testing the version of the game completed in that sprint to make sure it functions as desired. If you have several people testing your game and need to collate many reports of bugs or errors, consider providing the team with a method of logging and tracking issues that arise. Table 10-5 shows a sample error log.

The error log is a good methodology for tracking problems. Sometimes the fixes are placed into the next sprint, and sometimes they are delayed based on priorities. Keeping this type of log is useful whether you are creating a tabletop game or a digital game. In a tabletop game, the errors are likely to be related to game mechanics that didn't work as anticipated or an aesthetic that didn't resonate with learners. In a digital game, the log might track these things as well as actual functional errors, such as a swiping function that didn't work.

Table 10-3. Example of a Sprint in Game Development

Release 0.1: Login, Game Intro, Access to a Customer Type, and Overall Project Planning	Calendar Weeks	Points (Days)	CT Owner	Dev	Artist	Writer	Dev
Conduct planning meeting to refine release stories, define story cards, and refine story points across all sprints. Plan first eight map regions.		5.75	1.25	1.25	1.3	1	1
Create content worksheet template for a customer type.		0.5	0.25	0	0	0.25	0
Refine opening narrative, tutorial text, and description of customer type.		1.5	0	0.25	0	1	0.25
Finalize user interface design and create art assets and screen layouts for login screen.		11	1	3	7	0	0
Plan entire game map for all 40 regions; identify all building assets and their reuse. Sketch out up to 8 region layouts that can be reused with varying arrangements and coloring. Select starting stock images.	3 (January 11-29)	6.75	0.5	3	3	0	0.25
Program login, player actions for game start, and access to customer grid.		2	0	2	0	0	0
Complete testing and integration with customer learning management system.		2	0	2	0	0	0
Conduct client play-test of Release 0.1; identify revisions.		0.75	0.5	0.25	0	0	0
Subtotal build 1		**30.25**	**3.5**	**11.75**	**11.3**	**2.25**	**1.5**

Table 10-4. Example of a Build List

Tasks (April 30–June 1)	Hours	Completed
Game portal implemented (front end/back end) including user management training videos	10	
Scenario 1 dialogue revision: draft (client provides script)	4	✓
Scenario 1 linear revision: new dialogue quiz manager	5	✓
Scenario 1 linear revision: new dialogue quiz HUD	7	✓
Scenario 1 linear revision: revise game data, scenario manager, scenario action manager; new quiz responses	11	✓
Scenario 1 linear revision: revise NPC and player test	5	✓
Scenario 1 linear revision: new dialogue quiz questions and answers implemented	13	✓
Scenario 1 linear revision: Dirk AI controller and AI triggers	24	✓
Tutorial scene (7 part)	32	
Client doc inventory system: choose, weight, spawn, track collect, track points +/- when required	24	
Camera collider system: prevent wall occlusions	9	✓
Help UI (art supplied by interns)	8	
Leaderboard revisions	4	
Build Hours	**156**	

Table 10-5. Example of an Error Log

Who	Location in the Game	What Actually Happened	What Should Have Happened	Issue Repeatable
Joan	Unity player download	Error message	Downloaded	
Joan	Entering objectives—the directions are in the top entry box		Either move outside of the text entry box or have them automatically delete when you start entering data	

Having a process for rapidly testing and evaluating your game and then making changes will help you create the most effective learning game possible. The Agile process provides a great deal of flexibility and allows your team to adjust based on play-testers' reactions to the game.

Working With External Resources

Fortunately, you do not have to develop a learning game by yourself. If you look closely, you may have plenty of external resources at your disposal. One idea that many instructional designers overlook is to partner with a local college's game development program. Providing a real-world project for a class can often be a win-win situation: You will save money and students will gain valuable experience. The tradeoff is that the project process may be less polished than what you would get with a professional firm, and the quality assurance testing may be less rigorous.

For those with a bigger budget or access to an external learning game company, keep in mind that just because you are outsourcing development does not mean that you should not be involved with the process. External developers won't know your organization's culture or technical infrastructure. You need to be heavily involved in the play-testing, iterative design, and sprints to ensure that the learning game meets your organization's needs. If you have a passion for game design, you may want to be part of the initial brainstorming of the game design as well.

Wrap-Up

Developing a learning game can seem like a daunting task. However, if you approach development appropriately, the process can become more manageable. Once you gather your team together and choose your development tool, seeing progress after each sprint is exhilarating. Each version brings the game closer to release and closer to being played by the learners. The next chapter will focus on deploying your game and marketing it to potential learners.

Deploying Your Game

In This Chapter
✓ What logistical considerations should you plan for?
✓ How can you most effectively market your learning game?
✓ Two implementation case studies

A learning game is the same as any other learning solution you design: To produce results, you need to consider deployment as carefully as you consider design and development (Figure 11-1). Don't make the rookie mistake of assuming learners will be so intrigued by the idea of a game that simply getting to play captures their attention. You'll need a good implementation plan.

Figure 11-1. Learning-Game Design Process: Deploy

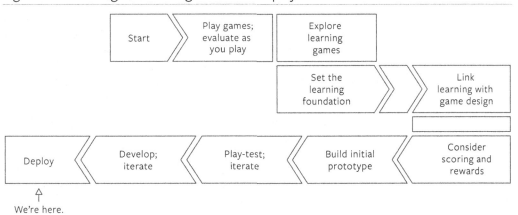

We're here.

Employees guard their limited time in the workplace. They feel constant pressure from competing demands: Emails, meetings, and deadlines all vie for attention. On average, employees spend about 33.5 hours a year on formal training endeavors (ATD 2016). This translates to about five minutes each workday available for training and development (Tauber and Johnson 2014). Because time is so precious, employees often regard training with suspicion. Most have experienced more than one training session that ended up being a waste of time.

Regardless of which statistic you focus on, either one indicates a need to create a comprehensive implementation plan if you want people to play your game. Your plan needs to include two primary elements: a logistics plan and a marketing and communication strategy. Let's look at each.

Logistics Plan

When preparing an implementation plan, learning-game designers tend to focus on logistics. Even so, they often underestimate all that goes into a comprehensive plan. You need to think through the who, what, when, where, and how of your game in a variety of areas. Depending on whether you are implementing a tabletop or digital game, these areas may include play-testing, facilitation, production, distribution and maintenance, usage, and game play. Tables 11-1 and 11-2 list questions your implementation plan needs to address for tabletop and digital games. We've provided the questions; your job is to identify answers for your specific situation.

Table 11-1. Logistics Considerations When Implementing Tabletop Learning Games

Consideration	Questions
Play-Testing	• Who should play-test your game as you develop it? How many play-testers do you need? (We recommend a max of four to six, although you may opt to use a different set of four to six people for each play-test.) • Who will recruit play-testers and how? What will you do with their feedback as you evolve your game? • How many iterations of play-testing can you include in your timeline? • Will you pilot your game? How much time will you allow post-pilot to make final revisions before launching the final version of the game? • Where will the play-testing take place? Do you want to record results to view later when making modifications to the game?
Game Production, Maintenance, Storage, and Shipping	• What game materials need to be created, ordered, packaged, and delivered? Do you need game boards, tokens, money, chips, cards, and so on? How will you get them? • Do you need to print materials? Where will you get this done? • Do you need to collate or assemble games? Who will do this? • How will you package your game so all components are organized and kept together? • Where will you store finished games and their materials? • How much lead time do you need to create, order, and package the games? • If games need to be shipped, how much time do you need to allow for shipping? (Hint: Assume a week's time if you are going coast to coast.)
Intended Use	• What is the intended use of your game? How do other decisions reflect this use? • Is it part of a workshop, in which setup and debrief instructions are incorporated into leader's guides? • Is it some sort of coaching tool for small groups, in which setup and debrief instructions need to be embedded within game materials? • Are you providing sufficient instructions given the intended use?

Consideration	Questions
Game Facilitation	• Will your game be facilitated as part of a workshop or training event? • Who will facilitate the game? Will it be you, another L&D professional, or a subject matter expert, who may have limited experience facilitating anything, let alone a game? • How will you prepare this facilitator to set up and debrief the game? Will you conduct a train-the-trainer session, or do you need to create a facilitator guide that can stand alone? Based on when your event is, when should you prepare your facilitators? (Too much time in advance and they will forget what you help them learn; too little and they will feel pressured.) • What type of facilitator guide do you need to create? Who is writing it? How will it be packaged and produced? • How will you make sure that the facilitator understands the learning design and the game play? • How do you ensure enough time for game setup, game play, and debrief? Do your instructions offer clear guidance on the time required for all three elements? • Do you offer guidance on what to do if the facilitator runs out of time?
Game Play Instructions	• How will people learn how to play? • Will you have players read your game rules from a booklet? • Will the facilitator explain how to play? • Will you create a video tutorial?

Table 11-2. Logistics Considerations When Implementing Digital Learning Games

Consideration	Questions
System Testing and Play-Testing	• Who will create and implement your test plans for experience usability? For play-testing of the game itself? • How will you do your testing? If your game is a mobile game, what tool will you use to distribute each release of your mobile app for testing? (At Bottom-Line Performance, we use a tool called HockeyApp, which enables us to mirror real-world use conditions.) How much time do you need for testing and iterating? • How many iterations of play-testing can you include in your timeline? • Will you pilot your game? What will the pilot plan look like? How many versions will you pilot before going to Release 1.0? How much time do you need for the pilot process? • Where will the testing take place? • Will you use any type of software to track play-testing results?
Game Distribution and Maintenance	• How will you distribute your game: a learning management system (LMS)? Online? A native app? • If you want to use a native app, do you need to pull game play scores into an LMS? If so, how will you do that? • If a web app, what browsers do you need to support? Who will maintain the game and address user-reported issues postlaunch? • If a native app, what devices and operating systems do you need to support? Who will maintain the game and address user-reported issues postlaunch?

Table 11-2. Logistics Considerations When Implementing Digital Learning Games

Consideration	Questions
Game Distribution and Maintenance	• If you are pushing out a native app, have you incorporated enough lead time for getting your app into Google Play or the App Store? (Apple typically takes much longer than Google. Allow yourself two weeks' time.) • Is there a plan to upgrade or update the game over time?
Intended Use	• What is the intended use of your game? How do other decisions reflect this use? • Is your game part of a live event? If so, when do you expect players to play—all at the same time or on their own throughout the day? Do you need to consider Wi-Fi availability? Will you have sufficient bandwidth for all the players you intend to have play? • If the game is part of an informal learning strategy, how do you get uptake and keep players engaged? • Are you providing sufficient instructions to managers whose employees will be playing the game? What are you doing for them to make sure that they understand what the game is about and how they can reinforce game play?
Game Facilitation	• How will you present the game to learners? Will they receive an email link? Will it be assigned to them from within an LMS? Will their managers inform them about it? • How will you build reflection time into the game play experience? Will there be some form of post-play debrief? Will this be a live event facilitated by players' managers? Will the time consist of postgame reflection questions? If so, how will you provide those reflection questions to players? • Is this game the entire learning experience, or is it part of something else, such as a live event? If so, how do you reference or reinforce the digital experience when doing the live experience? • If you have a facilitator, how will you ensure that this person understands the learning design and the game play? • How will you handle the introduction or tutorial for the game? Will it be embedded in the game? Will it be separate? • How much time will you give players to access and finish the game? How will you track progress and provide prompts if players do not access the game? • Is there a consequence for not playing? If so, what is it and how do you enforce it?
Game Play Instructions	• How will people learn how to play? Will you build in tutorials or provide explicit instructions? • Does your usability testing have a specific focus on making sure people can figure out how to play?

Marketing and Communication Strategy

Your marketing and communication strategy is the second part of your implementation plan. If your game is a tabletop game that is part of a workshop, your focus is on marketing the workshop. If it is a digital game, you usually are marketing the game itself. Even if the game is digital, be mindful that it will ideally be part of a larger curriculum for maximum effectiveness (Sitzmann 2011). Here are a couple of marketing suggestions.

Don't Make Your Game Optional

First, when setting out to market your game within your company, avoid using messaging that might suggest your game is optional. Your learners—busy employees—will translate that as "not really important to do." In fact, if your game will truly improve employees' performance, consider making your game play experience mandatory, especially if you have buy-in from senior leaders. The obvious exception to this would be a company marketing a public game or workshop that people choose to pay for and attend. We have included two case studies that outlines how you might market such an experience at the end of the chapter.

When we polled Knowledge Guru customers, we learned that companies that created Guru games and "recommended" people play had little participation. They tried using the enticement of "fun" (recall our warnings about this from earlier chapters), and found it was insufficient to make people believe the game would be a good investment of their time. Most employees do what's required, not what's optional. That's not a criticism of your employees or co-workers, but more of a general rule of the workplace.

Knowledge Guru customers who made the games a mandatory part of their learning solution usually found that the Guru game was the most highly rated portion of the learning experience. We found that the vast majority of learners who play a required Guru game say it is highly effective in helping them learn. Requiring game play will not be a negative for your learning solution if the learning experience proves valuable to your learners.

Second, create a communication campaign that includes several staggered messages delivered in a variety of ways. Once is not enough when communicating. Marketers have long assumed that seven to nine messages are required to convey a message (Smith 1886); you should assume a similar number is required for your message to stick. Here are several great tactics to consider:

- Posters that you can hang up in the workplace.
- Web banner advertisements that you can put on your intranet. Players can click the banner ad to gain access to the game if you are hosting it online. If it is an app available on Google Play or the App Store, link it to the app for easy downloading.
- An email drip campaign that sends a series of clever email messages over a period of days or weeks that encourage game play or alert people that something cool is coming.
- Weekly email updates regarding leaderboards and player stats.
- Small incentives that recognize performance. Consider featuring player profiles in a company newsletter, on a webpage, or in an email. You might also provide small prizes to game leaders, such as gift cards. Recognition from a senior leader within your organization can be a perk as well.

Implementation Case Study: A Paycheck Away

A Paycheck Away was created for the annual Indianapolis Spirit and Place Festival, which takes place over 10 days and features a different theme each year. Dozens of events are available to the public as part of this festival. Its goal is to promote partnerships between arts organizations, nonprofits, and businesses and use these partnerships to foster community discussions. The theme serves as the "umbrella" for the events that are part of it.

The 2012 theme was Play, and Bottom-Line Performance partnered with a local homeless shelter to design a game to help people explore the issue of homelessness. We involved the Central Indiana Chapter of the Association for Talent Development (CIATD) as "game masters"—facilitators who guided the entire game play experience—to make the game a success. The chapter also helped us secure a venue for playing the game. We could not make attendance mandatory, so we had to devise a marketing strategy that would draw people to our game. Here's how we got them there, and how we ensured flawless facilitation once they were on-site:

1. We wrote and published an educational blog series called "Games for Change" that detailed the game's creation as it was evolving. This series was targeted primarily to members of the Central Indiana L&D community. We began the series in July and published four posts between July and November 15, the date of the game event.

2. We created a website using the URL APaycheckAway.org, where we housed game materials and sneak peeks.

3. We created an extensive social media campaign on Twitter, scheduling an average of two to three tweets per day on living a paycheck away, homelessness, and our game event. To maximize reach, we created a Twitter account just for A Paycheck Away and then retweeted using our other Twitter accounts.

4. We contacted local news outlets and sent out press releases. One local paper did a terrific feature on the event.

5. We provided information on the event to the 15 game masters we trained from CIATD, as well as to the staff at Dayspring Center, the homeless shelter with whom we partnered. Each of these volunteers became a marketing voice for us as well, inviting their friends and neighbors to be part of the event.

6. We created a train-the-trainer session for all the game masters two weeks before the event—not too early and not too late. We had them first play the game and then practice being a game master. We made sure game masters had a written guide to reference while facilitating the experience. We also provided them with a copy of the game to practice with before the event.

The result was a sold-out event that was rated one of the best events of the entire Spirit and Place festival. Our campaign did its job—it got the butts in the seats. Game design quality and facilitation skills earned the high ratings. Pictures from the event are shown in Figures 11-2 and 11-3.

Figure 11-2. A Close-Up of the Game Board

Figure 11-3. A Game Master at the A Paycheck Away Game Event

Implementation Case Study: Zombie Sales Apocalypse

Zombie Sales Apocalypse is a game designed to teach sales representatives a sales process. The game has many technical implementation challenges because it was created in Unity 3D. The heart of the game is a branching simulation in which a player must make choices based on an interaction with a nonplayer character. The game was being released to a large insurance company and piloted among a group of its sales representatives. We had to overcome several technical and internal adoption issues to help ensure successful launch of the game:

- In the middle of development, Google announced that the Chrome browser would no longer accept plug-ins, which meant the game would no longer work on Chrome. The short-term fix for this was to switch to Internet Explorer until we could create a version that could run in Chrome.

- When Internet Explorer became our only choice, we had to request that IT allow players to download the Unity player to Internet Explorer. This request caused a massive delay, because security testing for the plug-in for the company was a major undertaking. It took weeks to finally get the plug-in approved.

- While the game was being developed, we faced a catch-22: We wanted play-testers to understand how to play the game, but until we nailed down a final design, we didn't want to spend time and effort creating a full-fledged tutorial. Our compromise was to create a PowerPoint-based temporary tutorial that we provided to play-testers so they could understand how to play the game and how to navigate within the environment. The PowerPoint tutorial proved very helpful and eliminated many questions.

- When we were in the pilot phase of the game, we did not have all the software connections to interface with the LMS. We had to decide whether to allocate our programming skills and time to creating an interface or focus on making the game as effective as possible. We decided that the best use of time would be spent on the game, but the client still wanted an indication within the LMS that the game had been played. Our compromise was to create a PDF document the player could access and open from the LMS (with the LMS recording the player doing so). The PDF provided a link to the game, which was housed on an external server. This meant that we did not need to go through an elaborate process to have IT vet the software and place it on their own servers. The cloud-based approach proved helpful.

- The play-testers for the second round of play-testing were geographically dispersed. We wanted to collect consistent data, so we pretested through the LMS what the players knew of the sales process. We then allowed them to play the game and had them complete a detailed play-test questionnaire related to the game. We collected these data using a survey tool and examined the data as they became available. We also post-tested the players using the LMS and measured the change in learning, which was statistically and practically significant.

- In terms of marketing, we had a bit of an uphill battle, because zombies are not usually viewed as the most corporate-appropriate approach to training. We created a whitepaper explaining the value of fantasy in learning and created a slide deck for our internal sponsors to promote the concept of the game to upper levels of management. Our primary internal champions scheduled one-on-one visits with members of the executive team to make sure that they understood how the game could provide valuable results, despite the zombie story and theme. The socialization process was a huge success, and prevented potential issues with the concept of using zombies for learning.

- One unplanned implementation element that worked to our advantage was the delay in the pilot caused by browser plug-in issues. The internal team was recruiting play-testers and building some momentum around the play-test process when the delays occurred. Because the team had been talking so enthusiastically about the game, the first group of play-testers could not wait to play the game. The delay heightened their anticipation, which, when combined with the limited number of play-testers, created a buzz around the game. When the game was released, the buzz drove participation and acceptance of the game.

Overcoming technical issues and promoting the game to company executives led to overwhelming acceptance and use of Zombie Sales Apocalypse. Several of the play-testers indicated that the game offered an engaging, interactive way to reinforce selling material, while still meeting educational needs.

Wrap-Up

A solid implementation plan considers logistics and marketing. It ensures that you are ready to roll out your game successfully and that people get excited about playing it. You worked hard to design and develop your game. Your implementation plan is the key to making sure your efforts are rewarded.

Final Thoughts

Congratulations! You now have a step-by-step process for creating an effective learning game, one that we use to create learning games for our clients and in the learning-game design workshops we conduct across the country and around the world. You can now set up a plan to develop your first learning game. With the lessons you have learned here, you should be creating high-quality learning games in no time.

As you can see from the chapters in this book and the amount of work involved, creating a learning game is not an easy task. Even though we have walked you through the process, you will continue to have opportunities to learn. No matter how many times we create learning games, we always learn from the process, and we keep honing our skills to create the most effective learning games possible. You need to do the same. Continue to play all types of games, continually develop learning games, try them out on learners, and revise as you learn what works and what doesn't work.

Take the time to make game play part of your weekly routine: not just game play for entertainment, but for study and growth. The more varied the games you play, the greater your ability will be to take a concept, idea, or subject and create a learning game.

Keep in mind that you should not create a learning game just to create a learning game. Instead, make sure that what you are creating matches the needs of the organization. And, never forget that the purpose of a learning game is to help players learn or reinforce knowledge. This purpose needs to be first and foremost as you design the game.

We wish you the best of luck, and have fun. But make sure your games are engaging and lead to learning!

Entertainment Game Evaluation Worksheet

What Is the Game Goal?

What Core Dynamics Were Used?

List at Least 3 Game Mechanics From the Game

Identify and Describe the Game Elements Used in the Game		
__ Aesthetics	__ Levels	
__ Story	__ Resources	
__ Chance	__ Rewards	
__ Conflict	__ Strategy	
__ Competition	__ Theme	
__ Cooperation	__ Time	

What Feedback Did You Get for How You Were Doing?

What Aspects of This Game Could Inspire Your Learning Game?

Other Notes

Entertainment Game Evaluation Answer Key: Plants vs. Zombies

What Is the Game Goal?

To protect your home from zombies; to defeat the zombies

What Core Dynamics Were Used?

The game combines various dynamics. Collection and Outwit are two big ones, particularly in early phases of the game. You collect sun, which enables you to choose resources that help you outwit and outlast the zombies.

List at Least 3 Game Mechanics From the Game

1. Different plants have different powers or capabilities.
2. Power-ups can be used to defeat zombies.
3. Giving your plants a dose of plant food gives them a temporary power boost.

Identify and Describe the Game Elements Used in the Game

Aesthetics	Levels	This game uses tons of game elements. The aesthetics, including sound, are really fun. There is a feeling of intense conflict or competition against the zombies as you try to outlast them. You progress through levels, with the initial levels helping you learn how to play and introducing you to new game elements as you go. Your resources increase as you play, giving you more options. You are rewarded frequently, and you can use strategy to decide how to place your plants. The zombie theme is exciting. Time is a huge element because you have to outlast the zombies in each round you play.
Story	**Resources**	
Chance	**Rewards**	
Conflict	**Strategy**	
Competition	**Theme**	
Cooperation	**Time**	

What Feedback Did You Get for How You Were Doing?

You either beat the zombies or they defeated you. You could see them progressing toward your house if you were unsuccessful in defeating them.

What Aspects of This Game Could Inspire Your Learning Game?

Zombies is always a fun theme! The idea of having to choose resources to serve as a blockade is also intriguing. The screen layouts themselves are useful to study to consider how you can have a graphically rich experience on a very small screen.

Other Notes

None

Learning Game Evaluation Worksheet

What Is the Game Goal?

What Is the Instructional Goal?

What Core Dynamics Were Used?

List at Least 3 Game Mechanics From the Game

Identify and Describe Game Elements Used in the Game

__ Aesthetics	__ Levels	
__ Story	__ Resources	
__ Chance	__ Rewards	
__ Conflict	__ Strategy	
__ Competition	__ Theme	
__ Cooperation	__ Time	

What Feedback Did You Get for How You Were Doing?

Other Notes

Learning Game Evaluation Answer Key: Password Blaster

What Is the Game Goal?

The goal of the game is to destroy bad passwords to earn as many points as possible. Shooting the passwords with the laser is engaging for many learners, as is trying to identify the correct password.

What Is the Instructional Goal?

The instructional goal is to distinguish between strong and weak passwords and identify what makes a strong password. Before playing, layers are given instructions describing weak and strong passwords. Whenever a player does something incorrectly, the game provides corrective feedback to help the player learn and correctly identify the password the next time.

What Core Dynamics Were Used?

This game is about aligning the laser to the incorrect password, so the core dynamic is alignment. You want to maneuver the laser once you identify the incorrect password so you can shoot it. The game gets faster the longer you play, so you must identify the passwords faster. This aspect is engaging and can be fun for many players.

List at Least 3 Game Mechanics From the Game

You lose points if you shoot down a strong password. You gain points by shooting an incorrect password. The more quickly you destroy weak passwords, the more points you earn. If you destroy a strong password or let a weak password go past, you lose a life. If you lose three lives, the game is over.

Identify and Describe the Game Elements Used in the Game

Aesthetics Story **Chance** Conflict Competition Cooperation	Levels Resources Rewards Strategy Theme **Time**	The element of time was critical: You only had so much time to identify and blast the incorrect passwords, and the game itself had a time limit. There was the element of chance—you did not know what type of password would be the next to fall. There was also the element of aesthetics—the look and feel of the game and the game elements was a little like an old-school arcade game.

What Feedback Did You Get for How You Were Doing?
You could track your point gains and also see how many lives you had remaining.
Other Notes
None.

Foundational Information for Game Design Document

Business Need

Instructional Goal
After playing this game, learners will:

Learning Objectives
To achieve this goal, learners need to be able to:

Player Persona
Constraints to Consider

Feed the World: Setup and Rules

Game Setup

- Lay the resource cards on the game board under the "Resources" label so everyone can see them.
- Place the scenario cards in the designated spot on the game board, scenario side up.
- Place the MSHA inspector cards face down on the spot labeled "Inspector."
- Place the year marker in the year one spot.
- Place the phosphate rocks in the area labeled "Food Bank."
- Place the seven spot markers on the circles on the game board.
- Place the team token on the first spot on the board.

Game Play

- The person who is first rolls the numbered die. This indicates how many scenarios the person needs to answer.
- The player reads a scenario aloud and then decides which resource card(s) need to be played to successfully respond to the scenario:
  - For example, if the scenario was, "You are about to enter a confined space to complete some electrical work," then the best resource cards to play are Process and PPE.
- The player then hands the scenario card to the person on his or her right. That person looks at the back of the card and tells the person whether he or she chose the right resources.
- The player then has to describe the specifics for each resource that is required:
  - For the same example, the player might describe what kind of respirator to wear, whether to complete a PJRA, and what kind of breathing monitor to take into the space.
- The person on the player's right provides feedback based on the answers on the back of the card. If the player has another scenario to answer, she or he does.
- The player is awarded one phosphate rock for each scenario answered correctly.

Place phosphate rock tokens in the column of squares above the current year. (Note: Phosphate rocks are not taken away for incorrectly answering questions.)

- When players reach year three, they must correctly respond to both the scenario and the challenge question (provided on the back of the card) to earn a phosphate rock. Again, no phosphate rocks are lost for incorrect responses.

- After the player's scenario(s) are answered, the player rolls the chance die. The player can gain an extra phosphate rock for good weather, can lose a phosphate rock if an incident is rolled, or may have to draw an MSHA card from the inspector deck. After resolving the results of the chance die, game play moves to the next player and the team token is moved to the next space on the board.

- Depending on how successful your team is at answering questions and rolling the chance die, it's possible to earn more phosphate rocks than are needed to meet the yearly goal. Extra phosphate rocks are placed in the lighter-colored squares in the column of the year your team is currently completing.

- The round continues until your team has visited all seven stops on the board. Then year one is over and no more phosphate rocks can be earned for the year one column. Begin year two by moving the year marker to the year two column and returning the team token to the first stop in the mine to market process on the game board.

- Continue game play until four years are complete.

Finishing the Game

The goal of the game is to complete all four years, earning an increasing number of phosphate rocks each year to feed the growing world population:

- Teams win a year when they have met or exceeded the phosphate rock goal for that year. The minimum yearly goals are as follows:
  - Year one: 5 phosphate rocks
  - Year two: 7 phosphate rocks
  - Year three: 9 phosphate rocks
  - Year four: 12 phosphate rocks

- The team with the most phosphate rocks of all the teams playing will be designated the overall winner.

Learning Game Play-Test Worksheet

Play-Test Questions	
Game Name:	Date of Play-Test:
What one word best describes your game play experience?	
What did you learn?	
How engaging was the game? 1 2 3 4 5 Not Super Engaging Engaging	
Did your engagement level change at any point during play (increase or decrease)? If it did change, why?	
What, if anything, did you find confusing or hard to understand as you played?	

What, in your words, was the objective of the game?
What information do you wish you had when playing the game?
Was there anything you didn't like about the game? What was it?
Final comments:

References

ATD (Association for Talent Development). 2016. *State of the Industry.* Alexandria, VA: ATD Press.

Barton, L.G. 1997. *Quick Flip Questions for Critical Thinking.* San Francisco: Edupress.

Boller, S. 2016. "BLP Partners With Mosaic and Ventana to Win Two Brandon Hall Awards." Bottom-Line Performance, September 15. www.bottomlineperformance .com/blp-partners-with-mosaic-and-ventana-to-win-two-brandon-hall-awards.

Brathwaite, B. 2012. Games for a Change. February 12, www.youtube.com/watch?v=y9Z -3mz3j6U.

Brathwaite, B., and I. Schreiber. 2009. *Challenges for Game Designers: Non-Digital Exercises for Video Game Designers.* Boston: Course Technology.

Cantador, I., and J.M. Conde. 2010. "Effects of Competition in Education: A Case Study in an E-Learning Environment." In *Proceedings of the IADIS International Conference for E-Learning,* edited by M. Baptista Nunes and M. McPherson. International Association for Development of the Information Society.

Connolly, T.M., E.A. Boyle, E. MacArthur, T. Hainey, and J.M. Boyle. 2012. "A Systematic Literature Review of Empirical Evidence on Computer Games and Serious Games." *Computers & Education* 59: 661-686.

Hays, R.T. 2005. *The Effectiveness of Instructional Games: A Literature Review and Discussion.* Orlando, FL: Naval Air Warfare Center Training Systems Division.

Kapp, K. 2012. *The Gamification of Learning and Instruction: Game-Based Methods and Strategies for Training and Education.* San Francisco: Pfeiffer; Alexandria, VA: ASTD Press.

Kapp, K., L. Blair, and R. Mesch. 2014. *The Gamification of Learning and Instruction Fieldbook: Ideas Into Practice.* San Francisco: John Wiley & Sons; Alexandria, VA: ASTD Press.

Lepper, M.R. 1988. "Motivational Considerations in the Study of Instruction." *Cognition and Instruction* 5(4): 289-309.

Malone, T. 1981. "Toward a Theory of Intrinsically Motivating Instruction." *Cognitive Science* 4: 333-369.

Nielsen, J. 2000. "Why You Only Need to Test with 5 Users." Nielsen Norman Group blog, March 19. www.nngroup.com/articles/why-you-only-need-to-test-with-5-users.

Sitzmann, T. 2011. "A Meta-Analytic Examination of the Instructional Effectiveness of Computer-Based Simulation Games." *Personnel Psychology* 64(2): 489-528.

Smith, T. 1886. *Successful Advertising: Its Secrets Explained.* London: Bazaar Press.

Tauber, T., and D. Johnson. 2014. "Meet the Modern Learner (Infographic)." Bersin by Deloitte, November 26. www.bersin.com/Practice/Detail.aspx?id=18071.

Werbach, K. n.d. "Gamification." Coursera course. www.coursera.org/learn/gamification.

Wouters, P., C. van Nimwegen, H. van Oostendorp, and E.D. van der Spek. 2013. "A Meta-Analysis of the Cognitive and Motivational Effects of Serious Games." *Journal of Educational Psychology* 105(2): 249-265.

Acknowledgments

Any book requires significant support from numerous people. *Play to Learn* is a truly joint effort, but we each brought unique experiences to it. We each have people we need to thank.

From Sharon

My spouse has to come first. Thank you, Kirk, for being supportive and positive and tolerating my stress when the deadline loomed, as well as for not complaining each time I bring home a pile of new games I want to play. Thanks to Steve Boller, Beth Boller, Kaitlyn Boller, and Nick Kirshner for always being willing to play a game.

On the professional side, I want to acknowledge all my teammates at Bottom-Line Performance (BLP) as well as some of our clients who let me share the games we created on their behalf. The work of these BLPers is represented within these pages. While I am fortunate to be the product owner for the Knowledge Guru platform and its suite of game-based apps, this platform is supported by a talented team of people who take and augment my ideas and produce amazing things from them. It's one thing to have an idea; it's entirely another for a team to take that idea and produce something from it. Brandon Penticuff, Corey Callahan, Jackie Crofts, and Bratt Conway are that team and they are amazing.

On the custom game development side, every game shown was a team effort involving many people. TE Town was produced by a large and talented cast of people. Laura Fletcher, Brandon Penticuff, Jackie Crofts, Jackie Lutzke, and Corey Callahan all played big roles. On the client side, a huge thank you goes to Diane Sweeney for working to secure permission for us to share TE Town in this book. I also want to thank Josh Kovalich, who has been an awesome project manager on TE's side, guiding us and getting us everything we needed. They both had a strong vision for how a game-based solution could benefit TE Connectivity, and they allowed us to partner with them in turning that vision into a reality.

A Paycheck Away was a labor of love for those involved because it was pro-bono work. Kristen Hewett, Steve Boller, and Matt Kroeger all collaborated with me to produce this game. Lori Casson and Cheryl Herzog of Dayspring Center in Indianapolis used their knowledge of homelessness and people who have been Dayspring clients to help us create a compelling game for change. Kristen, Matt, and Steve have also been faithful game masters, volunteering their time on numerous different occasions when Dayspring has hosted the game.

Feed the World was produced for The Mosaic Company. A special thank you goes to Andy McGuire for working with me to obtain permission to use this game as an example of good learning game design within the pages of this book. Thanks also to Linda Anhalt, who was the project manager on the employee onboarding and compliance training project that included this game. The team members who helped create this game included Jennifer Bertram, Sarah Owens, Jackie Lutzke, Jackie Crofts, and Corey Callahan.

Thanks to Dow AgroSciences, especially Marc Fisher and Karla Simpson, for granting permission to use the game image from Formulation Type Matters as well as information about the game. Thanks to Roche Molecular Systems for granting permission to share Viropolis game information and to Joni Zurawinski for helping us secure this permission.

Thanks goes to every BLPer who has played a game, and who has tolerated my enthusiasm for games and tendency to try to turn any activity into one.

Finally, thank you, Karl. You've been a terrific partner in writing a book and in facilitating workshops on games. I've said before that we are Oscar and Felix, and that works just great. From the moment we met in 2012, you've been a gracious partner and become a wonderful friend. I'd make a game with you any day.

From Karl

The process of writing is simultaneously an act of recording and discovery. As I write, I learn. I'd like to thank the following minds for contributing to my gaining of knowledge, starting with family. To my wife, Nancy, who is nothing short of wonderful; my two boys (Nate and Nick), whom I love and cherish; my mother, who taught me to love learning; and my late father, who taught me the value of hard work.

I'd like to thank the folks in Bloomsburg University's Department of Instructional Technology. I couldn't ask to work with better faculty and staff at any university. Special thanks to the students in the program, and to students everywhere whom I've had the honor and privilege of teaching and who have taught me so much. Teaching is a wonderful two-way street.

Special thanks to Bonni Scepkowsk, who is always so helpful; Jim Kiggens, who makes Zombies Sales Apocalypse and my visions of learning games a reality; and Justin Brusino, who helped to bring this book to life, along with Caroline Coppel and Jack Harlow.

Finally, a huge acknowledgment and thank you to Sharon Boller! Her love of games, enthusiasm for the industry, sense of organization, and willingness to harness my tangents makes her an awesome co-author and a wonderful person to work with for game development and workshop creation. Thanks, Sharon, it is always great working with you.

About the Authors

Sharon Boller

Sharon Boller is president of Bottom-Line Performance (BLP), a company she founded in 1995, which is currently in its second year on the *Inc.* Fastest 5000 Growing Companies list. She is the product owner of BLP's award-winning Knowledge Guru platform, which enables users to author and distribute game-based learning solutions. This platform earned the coveted Brandon Hall Gold award for best innovation in gaming and technology in 2014. Solutions generated from it have earned corporate partners Gold and Silver awards. In addition, BLP has earned numerous other awards for custom game-based solutions, including Horizon Awards, LTEN Awards, and Brandon Hall Awards.

Sharon partners with Karl Kapp in presenting the popular workshop Play to Learn: Designing Effective Learning Games for ATD LearnNow and for the eLearning Guild. She is also the author of *Teamwork Training,* and she wrote one of the chapters in Karl's *The Gamification of Learning and Instruction Fieldbook.* Additionally, she has written numerous articles, blog posts, and whitepapers on game-based learning, learning science, and instructional design.

Sharon frequently speaks on game-based learning and learning design topics at the local and international level for eLearning Guild, ATD, CLO, *Training* magazine, and other industry groups. She earned a master's degree in instructional systems technology at Indiana University.

Karl Kapp

Karl Kapp, EdD, is a professor, analyst, speaker, learning expert, and designer of instructional games and gamification. He is a full-time professor of instructional technology at Bloomsburg University, where he teaches subjects related to games, gamification, and learning technologies. He is the director of Bloomsburg's Institute for Interactive Technologies, which works with organizations to create interactive instruction, including games, gamification solutions, and simulations. Karl's work explores the research, theoretical foundations, and application of effective game-based learning. He is a TEDx and international speaker on the subjects of games, gamification, and learning innovation. Karl has served as a co–principle investigator on two National Science Foundation grants related to games and simulations, and has conducted research on a National Institutes of Health grant related to gamification.

Karl is founder of the educational consulting and game development firm The Wisdom Learning Group, where he consults internationally with Fortune 500 companies, government entities, and not-for-profit organizations in a variety of areas. This work includes helping them devise strategies around technology-based learning, game-based learning, gamification, instructional design, and learning technology strategy development. He is also co-founder of the educational games company 2K Learning.

Karl is passionate about sharing his knowledge and teaching others. To that end, he has authored or co-authored half a dozen books, including *The Gamification of Learning and Instruction* and *The Gamification of Learning and Instruction Fieldbook*. He has also authored several Lynda.com courses, including "Gamification of Learning" and "How to Increase Learner Engagement." Follow his widely read blog at http://karlkapp.com/kapp-notes or on Twitter @kkapp.

Sharon and Karl have traveled the country conducting private and public workshops based on the ideas and techniques within this book for many different organizations. Together they have helped many people create engaging and effective learning games.

Index